BEYOND THE BARS
FROM PRISON TO THE PODIUM

Chris "Tatted Strength" Luera

with Michael Oropollo

American Ghost Media, LLC

Santa Monica, CA

To Leslie
Thank You.
Thank You for the support

BEYOND THE BARS

FROM PRISON TO THE PODIUM

Chris "Tatted Strength" Luera

with Michael Oropollo

Published by
American Ghost Media, LLC
1305 Pico Blvd, Santa Monica, CA 90405
www.AmericanGhostMedia.com

BOOK DESIGN BY DAVID PISARRA

COVER PHOTO BY AMY GOALEN
www.AmyGoalen.com

ISBN 978-0-9831635-8-9

Some names, dates and locations have been changed to protect the innocent. Some individuals named are composites of real people.

This book is dedicated to my mother – without her undying love and efforts,
I never would have made it.

FOREWORD

I remember clearly the day that I met Chris Luera – he had that look of the newbie. It's a combination of excitement, awe, and nerves. He wasn't sure if he could join in and be a part of the calisthenics world. But I was sure we'd take him in – and I'm really glad we did.

Chris jumped in to our community with both feet – the way he does most things – there's no middle ground – it's all out from the get go. He learned quickly and before we knew it, he was teaching others the things he had been taught.

I've known Chris for 5 years now. I've seen him grow into a World Champion athlete, but also a World Champion person. We became very close while living and working in Dubai for months sharing an apartment. We'd stay up way too late, and he'd share his stories about life on the streets or in jail, and I'd marvel that the man I see in front of me, doesn't really resemble the man he was describing.

Today Chris is a professional speaker, trainer and most importantly, awesome father.

As I was reading this book, I couldn't put it down, which considering I'd heard about 80% of the stories already, says a lot to me about how enjoyable and entertaining this book is. I hope you get the chance to meet Chris after reading this book, and that you too become friends with the man that I am proud to know and call my friend – Chris "Tatted Strength" Luera.

Kenneth Gallarzo
Co-Founder – World Calisthenics Organization
Co-Creator – Battle Of The Bars

THANK YOU

I am so very grateful to so many people.

My father for his consistent encouragement and love. My sister Toni for always being there.

My wife who has stood by me through thick and thin and been a constant supporter of my goals and dreams.

Kenneth, Justin and all the men and women in Raw Movement who taught me calisthenics and welcomed me into their community. Yousuf and everyone at Gravity Gym who showed me Dubai and made it a life changing experience that opened my eyes to a whole new world.

Michael my co-writer, without his magical ability with words, I'd never have been able to express myself. The hours we spent together will always be remembered fondly by me.

Then there's David. If it wasn't for you, this book would never have been started, let alone finished. Your vision and determination made it happen. I appreciate all you have done to help me share my story. You pushed me when I needed support, and you reined me in when I needed grounding. Because of you I became a professional speaker. I'll be forever grateful.

Chapter One

They said I'd be dead or in jail by twenty-five. They were right about both. The old me died a long time ago, and he had to. The road I was on only led to concrete or pine boxes. Before I was Tatted Strength, three-time world champion calisthenics athlete – traveling, and teaching others the sport that saved my life – I was Chris Luera, gang member and convicted felon. The road from a drug addict criminal living on the fringe of society to world champion has been a trying and triumphant path. It is a mosaic of moments both beautiful and tragic and I have the scars, trophies, and ink to prove all of it. If you told me when I was eighteen years old that I would be where I am now, I would've laughed in your face and then tried to rob you.

I was born in Bakersfield, California, in 1986 to drug-addicted parents who put me up for adoption when I was three years old. I don't know much about my biological family. My mother's name was Robyn and I don't even know my father's name. I've never met them or seen them, but when I was younger my sister Danielle showed me two pictures of my biological mother. In one, she's a young woman, maybe eighteen or nineteen years old. She's wearing bell-bottom jeans, a button-down blouse with a wavy print and sharp lapels, and high heels. In the second picture, which was taken shortly after I was born and only a few years later, she is barely recognizable, beaten down from years of drug abuse. Those two pictures are the only relationship I have ever had with her.

The story of my parents is much like my own. They were drug addicts – junkies – running around the streets doing what people like us do out there. Their lives were periods of chaos followed by short bursts of getting their shit together for awhile. Then, inevitably, something would set them off and they would slide back into the drugs and the crime until it all came falling to the ground in pieces of burning debris. The final act for my mother came about when I was two or three years old. The short ending to her story is that she died of a drug overdose. Years later, during my first stint in prison, I learned more details of her death.

I was serving a twenty-month sentence for robbery and parole violations. At that point in my life no one in my family was talking to me except my biological sister Danielle. So few people wanted anything to do with me that when I got mail, I knew it had to be from her. She is seven years older than I am and separate families adopted us. When I was younger, she would come by my mother's house in San Pedro once a year and have lunch with me. We weren't close, but it was important to my adopted mother that I had some sort of relationship with my biological sister. I hadn't heard from her in years, but while I was in jail I took a shot and wrote her a letter. To my surprise, she wrote back. We got to know each other pretty well – as well as you can get to know someone through letters – and the topic of our mother came up. Danielle remembered details about our biological parents that I did not. After months of letters back and forth, I began to gather some of the missing pieces to an incomplete puzzle that I carried around with me everywhere I went.

The story goes something like this: My mother, father, and Uncle Bobby ran together in the same drug circles, getting high and committing crimes to feed their habits. The story begins the night my mother overdosed with all three of them together. Then there is a large gap in time, and it ends with my mother's body at the bottom of a cliff. No one knows if she was pushed, or if she fell. The details of that gap in time are murky and only the people who were there know for sure what happened. This occurred somewhere around 1988, and all three of them have taken that secret to their graves.

After my mother died my dad couldn't hold it together anymore. He dug deeper and deeper into his addiction and wasn't able to handle the responsibilities of taking care of two small children. He put Danielle and me up for adoption. Different aunts on our mother's side took us in.

I don't know what happened to my father after that. Everything I've heard is secondhand from Danielle and I'm sure she doesn't know the full story. Apparently, he continued to spiral down the path of drugs and crime until it killed him. I heard one story that he became a homeless vagrant who used to rob drug dealers, then I heard another about a drug dealer shooting him during a botched robbery, leaving him paralyzed.

That is the extent of my knowledge about my biological family. When I was young, the fact that I knew so little was a gaping hole in my soul that couldn't be filled. I wondered why they couldn't stop doing drugs when I was born, or why they put me up for adoption. I speculated and entertained fantasies around the night my mom passed away. They swirled through my head during sleep, school, at little league baseball games. It was an omniscient gust of wind that blew through my head and it created a pain and anger inside of me that I expressed through violence and drug use. I felt like

I had been given away, so I gave away pieces of myself to the drugs and the gangs with the hope that they would restore a feeling of wholeness to me.

The State of California was already familiar with my biological family throughout the years, as a result of drug use and constant police calls to our house for domestic violence and other disturbances. By the time I was put up for adoption, I was no stranger to the system.

I didn't spend much time in foster care and don't remember much about it other than our foster father always carried a gun on his hip, even around the house. I'm not sure what the gun was for, but it did not make me –four years old at the time – feel any safer.

My biological great-aunt and uncle, who I know as Mom and Dad, adopted me shortly after the foster care placement. Nancy, my adopted mother's sister, told Mom that my biological mother had passed away and that my father put me up for adoption. In the following days, my mother had a dream that she took me in. When she woke up, she said to my dad, "We are adopting Chris," and that was it.

My life has been blessed by moments of grace I can only describe as divine intervention. There's no logical explanation for why I am where I am today. The first act of grace I received was being adopted by my mother and father. They were much older and had already raised kids of their own. They could have retired well and lived happily and quietly for the rest of their lives. Instead, they chose to adopt a toddler and commit to the hard work that comes with raising a child, and for that my heart will be eternally grateful.

I spent the first night of my life with my new family at my sister Toni's house in San Pedro, a waterfront neighborhood in the southern end of Los Angeles. The next day I went to my parents' house, just up the block in San Pedro, which I would call home for many years.

My family has a long history in San Pedro, which is home to the Port of Los Angeles, the largest port in the United States. My family has worked on the docks for generations. My grandfather, Geronimo Antonio Luera, aka "Big G", worked on the docks and was one of the many who walked with Harry Bridges, founder of the International Longshore and Warehouse Union (ILWU). He participated in Bloody Thursday, the strike that started the ILWU. After that historical moment, he continued to be an influence in local politics, especially in matters relating to workers' rights. My dad, Alfred Luera Sr., dropped out of high school in the eleventh grade and went to work on the docks. He worked there for fifty years, from 1950-2000, an accomplishment and testament to hard work that makes me proud to bear his name. Before I went to prison for the last time, I never worked a full day at an honest job in my life. I couldn't comprehend how someone could stay in a job for fifty years. But that's my father's character, and that's the type of family I am proud to say I come from –hard-working, blue-collar people.

My first introduction to the rougher side of life was through the dockworkers my father worked with. The dockworker's persona reflects the work that they do. I was enamored by their grit and toughness at a young age. I saw them as real men, and I wanted the rugged and edgy persona they possessed. When longshoremen go on strike, it is always on a large scale and can be violent, a legacy of the Bloody Thursday strike that spawned their labor union. But when they talked, people listened and no one pushed them around. If they felt they were getting a raw deal, they fought back. When I was growing up, my father told me stories of going on strike and my mother cleaning houses to make enough money to hold the family over. The women were just as tough as the men.

My new sister Toni and brother Freddy were much older than I was and already had families of their own by the time I came along. We all lived in the same neighborhood, so growing up I always felt like I had a thousand eyes and arms watching and supporting me. I never felt alone. I always knew my family had my back.

Freddy's son Danny is technically my nephew but we were born only a few months apart. He was the closest thing I had to a brother. We played on the same sports teams, and were always the top two kids in our age group. When the other kids were still hitting balls off the tee, the coaches were pitching to us. That is how us Lueras get down. We strive to be the best at whatever we do whether we are working the docks or playing teeball.

One time Danny and I were shagging ground balls from my father in a contest to see who could get the most hits. The competition quickly got intense for two young boys. My dad got a kick out of this, and was egging us on, laughing under his breath when one of us got too heated. My father was chasing groundballs all over the field. The bar was being raised every at bat as we traded turns.

I went up to the plate, and set up in my stance totally focused on my dad who at this point looked labored over the whole thing. He pitched me a gem that came in slow motion right at the sweet spot – a little high and a little inside. I dropped the barrel on the ball and felt the sublime satisfaction only hitting a baseball perfectly can provide. The ball hissed through the air, took a skip off the dirt like a flat stone off water, and hit my father in the shin with a thud. He jumped in circles on one foot cussin' away while he held his leg. I stood frozen holding my aluminum bat while Danny burst into laughter. I felt bad for my dad, but he was a good sport about it, though he retired for the afternoon after that. Despite his age and my hyper-energetic personality, he always kept up with me.

Life was perfect and simple for me at that time. I was surrounded by love and support, and I felt whole. I didn't think about my biological family, or the chaos of my entry into the world. I was at peace. I never worried about anything. I had family on every block in San Pedro, and I felt secure wherever I went.

But that was short lived. I was soon to discover fear, insecurity, and discomfort. These emotions would be the driving forces behind many of the decisions I made over the next several years. The last day of summer always arrives quicker than we think. At some point, the vacation ends, and the real world begins.

When I reached the age of eight years old and ventured out into the larger world, I wasn't ready for it. I felt blindsided, as if one day I was picking dandelions in the outfield and the next I was thrown into the heat of competition. I felt like I was far behind everyone else, and we had just started this whole race of life. It was terrifying.

My first school was Holy Trinity Elementary School in San Pedro, a small Catholic school of only a few hundred kids, spread among grades one through eight.

I remember trying to read, and it felt like the words came alive and moved around the page. My thoughts would speed up, and I would begin to panic when I couldn't read words I saw other kids reading effortlessly. Teachers noticed my struggles and so did the kids, and I became the "slow, dumb" kid everyone would poke fun at to feel better about themselves. That first year, I was sent to a doctor who diagnosed me with severe ADHD and dyslexia. They put me on Ritalin, which didn't seem to help me in class, but I enjoyed its effects on me. It calmed me down and gave me focus. It also quieted the noise in my head – my relentless self-criticizer that echoed the negativity I heard from the kids who teased me and the teachers who were frustrated with me.

After a while, I resented school. This resentment, like most resentment, was driven by fear. I shut myself off to school, and accepted at the age of eight years old that I was not destined to succeed in this area of life. School brought to the surface internal issues and struggles that, until now, remained dormant. Socializing with strangers, trying to fit in with the other kids, learning how to share and play well with others, listening to teachers and doing school work – these were all new situations that I never dealt with before. They made me so uncomfortable that I began to reject the whole system. I didn't do well in math, but I excelled in defiance and rebellion.

Another uncomfortable and disheartening realization I had was the fact that my parents were much older than other kids' parents. My mom would pick me up from school, and as I would walk to her old silver Toyota Camry, I would notice kids staring at her with a puzzled looks. After a few weeks the questions came: "What happened to your mom? Why's your grandma always picking you up?"

For a while, my reply was, "My mom got eaten by a lion." That always ended the conversation. The look of shock and fright on their faces gave me the satisfaction of a small victory. But then the kids told their parents what had happened to my mom. Teachers told my parents, and both scolded me for making up this story. They told me that I was being a troublemaker. Now I was a troublemaker! Really, I was just acting out from the pain of being different, of not fitting in, of being adopted, and of not knowing what happened to my biological family. I continued to stuff that pain deeper inside of me and began to act out more frequently.

My mother was very active in school – more so than most parents who just make their kids lunch and send them off into the wild. She helped with school activities by chaperoning field trips and helping out during lunches and book fairs. One of those school activities was Hamburger Tuesday. She would help serve hamburgers at lunchtime. Hamburger Tuesday was a big deal at Holy Trinity. Everyone – except me – looked forward to it. But I was, and still am, a picky eater. I couldn't stand hamburgers. This did not boost my popularity, as Hamburger Tuesday was the one thing that every kid in the school agreed was awesome. Now I was also the only kid in the school who didn't like Hamburger Tuesday. I couldn't get anything right.

Every Tuesday my mom would pack me a separate lunch, and I would be the only kid eating pizza. One of those Tuesdays I sat down for lunch with a table full of kids, and one of them blurted out curiously "Is that your grandmother?" My heart sank into my stomach. Those questions made me want to crawl out of my skin with discomfort. Looking down at my lunch, the only lunch in the entire cafeteria that wasn't a hamburger, I said "No, that's my mother." The pizza, the mother that people thought was my grandma, the learning disabilities they all folded and crashed into me at once. It was a microcosm of my experience during those early years at Holy Trinity. They became the foundation for the rest of my life. Not too long before, I was the happy, carefree kid playing baseball in the park. I shelved those experiences and chalked them up as a dream state fantasy. I guess I figured that life would never be beautiful like that again – that it shouldn't be. I learned that life was a struggle, and mine was just beginning.

My parents loved me deeply. They were present, active parents who put in the time it takes to give a kid the best shot at life. I know in my core that they never felt I was a burden. There were countless days I dragged my father outside to play catch or hit baseballs, or make him show me how to box. The living room saw more scraps than Madison Square Garden. And my mother had eyes in the back of her head. She was always nearby, and quick to drop down the hammer of discipline on me when I was out of line. I would be doing something I wasn't supposed to be doing, fully confident I was alone, and she would appear out of nowhere, with a broom, spatula, or her hand to shoo me off with. But she made our house a home, and took care of the family.

As I got older, anger and mischief blossomed in my fertile soil. Several years of being bullied and not fitting in hardened me. I began to walk down a more serious path of defiance, trouble, and violence. It was clear to my family that this was not merely a stage. These traits were becoming part of my character as I shed the softer, carefree side of myself that I possessed in childhood.

Around the age of eleven I discovered chemical substances other than Ritalin that I could use to change the way I was feeling. At that age my access to drugs was limited, so I used the only drug that was readily available– computer cleaner. I started huffing computer cleaner with some frequency because it made me feel goofy, and it melted away those insecurities and fears I carried around. I was finally able to get out of my head, which was always a loud place.

I quickly discovered pot and alcohol. I had to go through friends or their older brothers to get it, but whenever I could, I did. I got high on whatever was available, and became more brazen with my drug use to the point where I was huffing computer cleaner while in anti-drug D.A.R.E class. I'd take a hit of the duster in between learning the dangers of huffing chemicals. It was only a matter of time before I got caught, which I did when a girl saw me huffing the cleaner in class. She immediately reported me to our principal, Ms. Wiley.

They called me into her office and searched me but found nothing. But they were onto me. But all those years of being a black sheep trained me to hide from the inevitable trouble that was coming my way. I was a problem kid. I didn't do well in school. I could never focus on anything, and I loved getting into mischief. I spent as much time in detention as I did in class, but I learned how to play the cat and mouse game well, and became comfortable in my role as the mouse.

A few weeks after the incident in D.A.R.E. class, a campus officer and Ms. Wiley took my backpack while I was at lunch and searched it. They found bottles of computer cleaner and hauled me into Ms. Wiley's office again. She said, "This is the end of the road, Chris. No suspension for this one. I have to call your mother. This is grounds for expulsion." "Expulsh-!?" I tried to protest. "Drugs!" she said as she slammed the bottle of cleaner on the table.

What Ms. Wiley didn't know was that I had an ace up my sleeve. My street instincts were developing, and I knew a few basic things like always have an alibi. I said "Call Ms. Herrera!" and so she did. Ms. Herrera told Ms. Wiley that I came into her computer class and offered to bring in extra cleaner from home. Ms. Wiley was dumbfounded, and I had a shit-eating grin on my face, until she asked Ms. Herrera, "When did Chris tell you this?" "About fifteen minutes ago," Ms. Herrera replied. I went white from head to toe. I was street smart, but I was still young and sloppy. Ms. Wiley had me at checkmate. I was expelled from Holy Trinity in the middle of seventh grade.

Since I was kicked out in the middle of the school year, my mother came up with a plan to keep me out of trouble. I wasn't home for a week when she said, "So you have two choices.

They can hold you back, and you will have to repeat seventh grade again, or you can complete the rest of the year's work at home."

I remembered how bad things were after I repeated the second grade at Holy Trinity. I had to make new friends and endured tortuous bullying. I was going to finish the seventh grade no matter what it took. Every week my mother gave me stacks of work packets, and I completed them diligently. I would forgo hanging out with friends and running around the streets. I put everything I had into completing the work, because under no circumstance was I going to get held back again.

As summer came around, I was ecstatic when I found out I would be graduating and would not have to repeat the year. I would've graduated anyway, regardless of whether I completed those packets or not. Where did those packets go after I labored for hours every week completing them?

The trash.

My mother conjured up the story of being held back and created those packets – at least fifty of them – to keep me off the streets and out of trouble. She was slick, and it worked.

When I started getting into trouble my parents had opposite responses. My father was the laid back parent, while my mother was the disciplinarian. Dad was the type of parent who would give me money or cigarettes when I was strung out and broke. When Mom kicked me out of the house, he would leave the garage door open at night so I wouldn't have to sleep outside. My mother on the other hand was tougher than most of the guys working on the docks. She didn't put up with my insane way of life, and came down hard on me when I began screwing up. There was no hesitation on her part to call the cops on me when I was out of line. I needed the soft approach of my father and the tough love from my mother. They balanced one another.

My parents developed their different styles as a result of their pain from the death of my Uncle Jimmy. Jimmy was my blood uncle who, like me, came from a family of drug addicts who were in and out of prison. After his dad went to prison for the final time, my family took him in.

Uncle Jimmy was a legendary sports star in our area. My father would talk about his athletic skills like it was ancient folklore. When his biological father got out of prison, Jimmy went back to live with him. My parents were devastated and begged him to stay. But he was troubled, like I was, and made up his mind to go live with his dad.

He died of a drug overdose shortly after. This crushed my folks, especially my father. I could hear the pain cracking in his voice when he told me stories of Jimmy's athletic achievements. If you compare our stories, they are eerily similar. The only difference is that I was given a second chance and he was not. I'm not sure why. I guess it could be as simple as the luck of the draw. Now, looking back, I empathize on a deep level with what my parents had to go through raising me. It was like they were reliving the horrors of my Uncle Jimmy with me, watching the same painful scene playing out again. They knew they could not control this kind of ride – it was over when it was over.

***

After that summer I began eighth grade at a school in Ranchos Palos Verdes. We had a relative who lived in Palos Verdes and used their address to get me into the public school in this affluent area of Los Angeles, northwest of San Pedro.

My mother was especially happy I was going to school there. I was smoking weed and drinking on a daily basis. It was obvious my life was gaining momentum down the wrong path. She was desperately trying to do what she could to keep me out of trouble. Mom wanted to keep me away from the drama and street politics that was just beginning for boys my age in the San Pedro middle schools.

When I heard I would be going to school in Palos Verdes, the gears in my brain started turning. I began scheming ways I was going to make money and those kids had money. I would be the guy from San Pedro who could get them anything they couldn't get their hands on in the suburbs.

I became fully committed to selling drugs. I would skip class, smoke weed, and sell it to support my habit. The campus was a sprawling indoor/outdoor complex, which made it easy to hide in the shadows and avoid getting caught. After two months I was called into the principal's office. I was getting good at the cat and mouse game and was much less sloppy than my rookie years at Holy Trinity, so I knew it wasn't for selling weed.

The principal found out I did not live in Palos Verdes. He called my mother, and I was expelled for the second time. I would have to go to Dodson, the public school in San Pedro where all the neighborhood cats I ran with went. Dodson was the school my mother was trying to avoid. It was a place where the kids were just like me. We had the same street mentality.

Chapter Two

Dodson was wild, straight up. It was a rough group of kids from all over the San Pedro area. Rivalries, gang ties, and vendettas carried from the schoolyard to the street. It was my time to break out. My mother couldn't shelter me anymore. I was ready to let the tide of the streets pull me in.

The teachers couldn't handle the students. and left us largely to govern ourselves. They did their best trying to teach the students who wanted to learn, but they were just scenery, like a desk or a chair. Kids from the same neighborhood stuck together, and stuck up for one another. The schoolyard was as segregated as the prison yard, and there were fights every day. On Thursdays, the students would congregate behind the baseball field after school to watch that week's drama get settled with fists, like they were sitting ringside at the Forum. For me, I had finally found the camaraderie and friendship I'd always wanted. I was no longer a loner, an outcast.

My second day at the school I got into a fight with a kid from a rival town. Far from being scared, I loved every minute of the action. I was drawn to the adrenaline rush of it all – the buildup and the trash talking, the short bursts of combat followed by the resolution one way or another. I was just drawn to the violence. It didn't matter if I was a bad student, and didn't fit into the neat social structure of the law-abiding society that Holy Trinity represented. At Dodson, I fit in because I could fight and hustle. I was a part of the crowd. I belonged.

We were nearing the end of eighth grade and preparing for high school, but we acted a lot older than we were. We spent a lot of our time hanging out with our friend's older brothers, trying to learn as much as we could about the way this world worked. They were in high school, sometimes older, and many of them were affiliated with the local gangs.

I always wanted to be famous. When I was younger, I wanted to be a football star or a baseball standout like my brother Freddy. As I entered my adolescence, I wanted to be known as a gangster, the guy people whispered about, who they feared when I got out of prison. I would always hear the older kids talking about those guys.

"Things are going to be different when he gets out of the pen."

"Everyone is going to have to be on their best behavior. He doesn't play around."

I dug deeper into the underbelly of the streets. I rarely had to look for trouble; it was always right in front of me. I was drinking and using drugs on a daily basis. The neighborhood guys and I started committing crimes with deliberate criminal intent rather than with schoolboy mischief. We were selling weed, committing petty thefts, and tagging buildings with graffiti.

I especially loved tagging because of the permanence of it. All the neighborhood taggers had their own unique style and signature. When someone drove by your tag, they knew you did it. It became a goal and a game to tag the most areas in San Pedro, and the hardest ones to reach, like billboards and high up on building walls.

Every neighborhood had a tagging crew with its own logo or saying that they would spray-paint on the side of buildings. Crews would get into beefs with one another and tag over each other's logos. When two beefing crews met up or walked by each other in the hallway, it got violent.

My first arrest was for tagging. I was twelve years old. I didn't think anything of it. It was just a graffiti arrest. But when I came into school the following Monday, I found out my friend Jeremy's mom had signed him up for a boot camp for troubled youth with the Sheriff's Department because of the trouble he was causing. I begged Jeremy to tell his mom not to say anything about the camp to my mom, but I was too late. When I went home, I was signed up too. No amount of pleading worked to get me out of it.

The boot camp was my first experience with the criminal justice system. The camp was held Saturday mornings and once a week after school. It was your typical Marine-style boot camp - they tore us down to build us back up. My mother would always drop dimes on me to the drill sergeants about my bad grades or the trouble I was getting into. They rode me extra hard. Nevertheless, I continued to get in trouble and fail drug tests for pot. They nicknamed me "loser" because I failed so many drug tests. The deputies wrote me off as another lost cause they would have to deal with on the streets in a couple years.

Later that year, while I was on probation for one of the many tagging arrests I racked up, I came home drunk and ended up in a screaming match with my mother. She threatened to call the cops, so I grabbed her keys and stormed out of the house. I stole her silver Camry, picked up my buddy, and we were off running. I was out of my mind at this point. When I picked up my friend, I was driving like a maniac and enjoying the thrill of it. He was not. He begged me to pull over and let him out of the car.

"Fine get out and walk," I barked.

He split, and I roared off down Sepulveda Boulevard.

As I tore down the street the back of the car fishtailed, and I felt the unique euphoria that comes with screaming tires and the smell of burnt rubber. I pressed down on the gas pedal, took a turn too fast, and crashed my mom's Camry into a row of parked cars.

"Shit."

Panicking, I got out of the car, and sprinted from the scene. About half a block away, I stopped and remembered that the car I crashed was my mother's, so I ran back and drove the car home. The sound of mangled metal was horrendous, and the car screeched all the way into my parent's driveway. I got out of the car, took a look at it, and turned around into my father's chest. He was standing in the driveway waiting for me.

He cussed me out and hit me. It was one of the only times he ever laid a hand on me. I fell over and passed out from the adrenaline. When I came to, I was in the back of a cop car on my way to booking. This would be my first long-term trip to juvenile hall, where I stayed for five months. That was where I got my first look at the L.A. gang scene.

I walked into the Los Padrinos juvenile center terrified. The place was like a real prison in its structure and overall feel – the cells, the overcrowding and the violence. Padrinos was also the first correction center where I saw steel bars. They jarred my reality – an immovable symbol of permanence and hopelessness that disturbed me. But I was not behind bars just yet. The overcrowding was so bad that forty of us had to sleep on the day room floor.

Around a month into my stay I went to the infirmary to take my medication. I ran into my floor mate Nasty.

"So what set you belong to?' he asked.

"What do you mean?"

"Like what gang you rep, fool?"

"Me and my friends have a tagging crew. That's why I'm here, I keep getting popped for tagging."

"A tagging crew?" He laughed at me, wondering if I was telling a joke or if I was really that naïve.

"Man, you need to get cliqued up with a gang. No one cares about your little tag crew. They'll eat you alive, bro. They fuck with dudes who aren't cliqued up, man."

Life on the day room floor was tough, especially because it was so crowded. Fights were constant, and after remaining under the radar for a while, I got caught up in the violence. Everyone does eventually. The fight was with one of the gang kids over something I can't even remember. I am sure it was trivial and meaningless. The kid squared up with me and as soon as I put my hands up, my head was bouncing back and forth like a punching bag. I didn't even have time to gather myself. The whole fight lasted about thirty seconds, and it was clear I lost.

When the guards broke it up, they put us both in the box. That's the juvenile hall version of the hole. I began to flip out in there, kicking and punching the door and walls. I was cussin' out every guard that walked by. One guard eventually got sick of my relentless verbal abuse. He came up to the cell, opened the door, squirted a tiny bit of pepper spray in my eye and walked away. I keeled over in pain. Knowing I deserved it and not wanting to experience that again, I kept quiet from then on.

They treated us like adults in there, and no one cut us any slack because of our age. The structure of juvenile hall and the treatment from the guards is enough to start hardening any kid into a criminal.

***

I got out of Los Padrinos a week before high school registration. Registering at San Pedro high school was the first order of business my mother had in store for me. San Pedro High School is roughly three or four thousand kids. It is so big that the front of the school starts on 14th street, and the back of the school ends on 17th street. It is an old style, drawn out, large campus. It has been used for shooting in several movies, especially skateboard films, because of its large staircases. I thought game on – girls, fighting, selling drugs. I couldn't wait.

I knew high school was going to be wild. You start fantasizing about the parties and the girls when you are in seventh and eighth grade. I was excited and had everything ready for my first day. I dressed in the flyest clothes I owned at the time, with crisp white Nike shoes, and brought my little weed pipe I carried with me everywhere.

The first day I was completely overwhelmed. I immediately caught on that I should never bring my pipe to school. There is campus police everywhere. But everyone was smoking weed. In middle school there was only a small percentage of kids getting high and partying. Now, everyone was doing it. I'd skip homeroom to smoke, then run into someone else on the way to class who needed a bowl, and I'd skip first period to go smoke with them. This would continue all day – crossing paths with different people and getting high. There was a lot of money to be made here. I started selling weed to everyone, and people began to know me.

San Pedro High was just a new venue for the criminal activity I was already partaking in. It was a new means to the trying to do drugs, trying to sell drugs, trying to be a badass that I was caught up in. Pedro high was a concentration of people my age – it was where everybody was at, the girls, the druggies, the parties – and I was getting recognition. Or I felt that I was getting recognition. It wasn't like the movies where the kid walks into school and everyone in the hallways stops to look at him. But in my mind, I was already becoming a legend. My young damaged ego began to swell with pride of what I thought I was. I was hanging out with the senior guys, the senior cheerleaders. As a freshman, the coolest kids in high school were accepting me because I did drugs and sold them drugs. It was fun, and for three months I had the time of my life. But I was moving way too fast and got myself busted by the police. I was shipped off to juvenile detention once again.

This wasn't my first go around at this incarceration business. Los Padrinos gave me a quality education in what was to be expected from the guards, prisoners, and myself. Honestly, I was cool with it. At the time, I even enjoyed it. I loved the chaos of it – the spontaneous fights in the hallway because two enemies crossed paths, or because someone talked shit to the wrong person. The chaos is what drew me in to the criminal life.

My second stay in the detention center was a breeze. I felt like I was enrolled in higher learning of being a criminal. I did my bid up there with no problems and was released. Once again, I would have to register for school. I always knew the importance of a high school diploma. I did not know why, but I just knew that I had to be in school. I figured that if I aimed for the diploma and failed, I could at least get my GED.

Other kids get out of juvenile hall and they have the mindset that they are already grown men. "Why would I go to school? Why should I go to school?" But that was never my mindset. I always wanted to graduate, even though I never applied myself. I enjoyed going to school. Not necessarily to do the schoolwork, but because of the social scene – the girls and friends. That's where they all are. I saw school as a fun place to be.

When I got out, I went to register. They told me I couldn't come back because I just got out of juvie, and instead I'd have to go to a probational school. Probational school had like 25-35 kids in it. Most probational schools are set in office buildings. You would never even know it was a school. You stay there all day, from morning til afternoon, and you don't leave until the day is finished. That place was even crazier. Out of 30 kids, at least 26 of them were getting high and running around the streets.

When I got out of juvie, I also went back to tagging with my crew, but I wasn't the same kid. The violence and gang mentality changed me. That conversation with Nasty in Los Padrinos a year ago changed me. It stuck in my head all this time and solidified after my second trip to juvenile hall. I wasn't going to be the odd man out, the punch line to anyone's joke, or anybody's prey. Gangs ran everything, that was a truism to me, and I wanted to be a part of that world. I became committed to the streets. I told myself that these were not childish games played among kids anymore. This was the for real now, and I was going to shape myself to fit the mold.

I brought back to the streets with me the organization of the gangs in the juvenile centers I was in. My niche was the tagging and graffiti scene, which was the minor league in the gang world. Tagging crews are organized and operate much like gangs, but don't partake in a lot of the violence street gangs do. I soon organized a well structured tagging crew that operated all over Los Angeles. We became a player in the scene – no longer written off as a collection of neighborhood misfits. As the head of the crew my name caught recognition, and I rose through the ranks of the L.A. tagging underworld. I got the respect and notoriety I always wanted. It was not on the scale of the big time gangsters I idolized, but I was on the path.

The only thing that means anything in the tagging world is notoriety. We paint murals of our name on buildings. The bigger the mural, the more fame you and your crew receives. For me, a kid who always held romantic ideas of being a famous gangster, I felt like I was getting closer to that fantasy. But I was growing out of the role of graffiti artist. My propensity towards violence and serious crime was far outside the boundaries of a tagging gang.

I traveled all over Los Angeles collaborating on projects with different crews. The people I met were ghosts – appearing, disappearing, and reappearing after weeks or months. Some went to prison; others got caught up in drugs. The scene was a constant revolving door of faces and crews.

One of the guys I met along the way was Spider. He was an elite tagger and a well-respected member of one of the biggest crews in the city. His artwork can still be found all over Los Angeles. Some of that work I collaborated with him on. The guy was a superb artist whose skills we all held in high regard. I knew Spider long before we became taggers; I grew up down the street from him. When we were in middle school – riding around in skateboard crews – we would see each other around town, although our interactions were limited. Now we stumbled into the same circles once again.

He was about five or six years older than me and I looked up to him. He was a terrible role model by my current standards, but as a young teenager I had a different idea of what a role model should be, and he was it. He had access to money, women, and drugs. When he took me under his wing, I felt honored. I knew he would give me an advanced level of schooling on the streets.

As an up and comer, I was always looking to push the limits. I had a chip on my shoulder and I wanted to be running to home base when everyone else was still on their way to first. Part of that deal was being the first out of my friends to try hard drugs. To others I was the guinea pig, but I didn't see it that way. I saw it as the first step towards earning my stripes – my street credibility. Spider was the first person to introduce me to crack cocaine while everyone else was still smoking pot. My desire to be the baddest guy on the block overrode the fear of everything I heard about drugs growing up. The introduction to hard drugs would permanently tilt the axis of my life. I finished my school year at the probational school and with that finished, most of the formal education I would ever receive. I would stay enrolled throughout various high schools, in between stays at correctional facilities, but I was just a name on a class roster. I never attended.

***

Spider and I just finished painting a piece one summer's day. It was dusk and finally starting to cool down. He went home to chill out for the rest of the night and I told him I'd link up with him after I ran a few errands.

I met him over at his place. He lived in a run-down, one bedroom apartment on the east side of town, along with his girl, their two cats, and a couple transients on any given night. The house smelled like stale beer and cat piss, which even the overwhelming smell of cigarette smoke couldn't cover up. I looked into the living room. Some of the guys were playing video games. Spider was sitting on the couch behind a pile of cocaine, smoking out of a pipe.

I was six to ten years younger than anyone there. I was terrified, but doing my best to keep it together and look tough. Those feelings generally sum up all of my experience before I decided to turn my life around. It was like when you are a kid jumping off cliffs into the ocean. You are staring over the edge of the cliff, terrified, but your friends are cheering you on. The voice in your head says, "Fuck it, just jump." That's how I felt my whole life.

Spider wasn't smoking weed. It didn't smell like pot. It smelled like burnt chemicals or plastic, but it wasn't overwhelming.

I assumed he was smoking the cocaine. I greeted everyone with a nod and sat down next to Spider. I was curious as to what was in the pipe, but I wouldn't dare ask, I'd look so stupid. I hung back, sinking into the couch and watching the guys play video games. Spider's closed fist lazily hit me in the chest. I looked down at his hand, which was clutching the pipe, and looked up at him. His head was straight, but his eyes were staring off somewhere distant. He turned to me. "Do you want a blast?" His eyes looked wet and glazed over. His pupils were pinheads. His face looked like it was made out of rubber. He looked terrible.

I didn't want to try. I could see how bad this was. Even in my naiveté, I was aware that if I took a hit off that pipe, the course of my life was going to be altered. But the voice in my head said, "Fuck it, just jump."

"Yeah, let me hit that." The words somehow rolled off my tongue, and without a breath of hesitation. Spider gave me a stoned half-smile and shot out of the depths of the couch into an upright position. He packed the pipe full of rock cocaine and handed it to me. He told me to take a big hit and hold it. I fired up the pipe and ripped it with a lungful of air. I held the smoke deep in my lungs and looked at him with a blank expression and my cheeks puffed out.

"Do some pushups!" he yelled. I dropped down and starting banging out pushups. Before I could finish a set of ten, I got up to my knees and blew out the smoke. I looked around and it sounded like a train was roaring through my head. I felt like I had just been hit with a right hook in the mouth. I was flying and I loved every second of it. A piece of my soul went into the pipe that night, another small piece of myself given away.

Graffiti is a costly trade. Paint is expensive, and you can never have enough paint. Tops with varying nozzles that manipulate paint thickness are needed. Then, there are the fines and bail a person tallies during his tagging career. It all racks up to a costly way of life. I couldn't print money fast enough to keep up once I added a crack habit to the mix. I was sixteen years old. I didn't have a job, nor was I capable of working any sort of mainstream, socially acceptable gig. I was as much a part of the streets as the bricks I was painting over at night.

I was a great thief though, and as a creature of habit, I went to what I know. I would steal paint from every art store in San Pedro to keep my tagging reputation intact. A tagger with no paint is like a writer without a pen. But my crack habit went from a disruption in my life to becoming my life. I became tired of having to steal paint – and having to steal everything else to fund my habit. From that first hit at Spider's place, I was hooked. I began smoking every day. Crack brought me down to a new level of criminality with elements of danger and desperation that I'd never experienced before.

I became less of a tagger and painter, and more of a fiend. I spent less time tagging with my crew, instead deciding that we needed to expand to other areas of crime, specifically theft. A small subgroup of our tagging crew developed a primitive but effective theft ring. We targeted electronic stores, stealing DVDs and CDs. Then we resold them to street vendors or bootlegged them ourselves.

There was nothing sophisticated about our theft ring. It was a very crude, smash-and-grab type of operation. I would walk into an electronics store with a backpack, stuff it full of DVDs and CDs, and run out of the store at full speed until I was far away. Stores began to get wise to the backpacks and made people leave them at the front door. To counter this, I wore an extra coat and pair of pants that I stuffed with products. When they added security strips to the cases, I stole the security key that disabled it.

We were stealing a lot of inventory, and it still was not enough to fund all of the drugs and partying. Truthfully, it could never be enough. There was no such thing. I just knew at that point that I was done tagging. I was hanging out with my crew less and less. My primary concern was stealing enough odds and ends to keep my crack habit funded one more day. Graffiti was now just a childish petty crime that didn't earn me enough street cred and cost too much money.

Chapter Three

A storm had been gaining strength inside me. It was cold and black, and I, tethered to nothing, was at its mercy.

Johnny was an old friend of mine from Dodson that lived on a San Pedro block popping with gang activity. At any time of the day or night, the block was alive with a dark electric current. Runners were running – drugs, women, information. The good ol' boys were perched on stoops, looking out for business and threats, customers and cops, friendlies and rival members, ready to turn the block into a warzone at the first signs of the enemy.

Me and my homies Johnny and Jeremy, the three of us, plus a few others made up our core group. We became inseparable. I linked us up with some of my old tagging crewmembers, and we had a solid clique to run with. We were in the heart of the action and I felt like I had finally arrived somewhere. I was a part of something that mattered. I belonged to a scene and culture that was much bigger than I was.

Gangs are split up by turf, with boundaries drawn according to the blocks that neighborhood cliques live on. Johnny's block was part of the same gang.

Johnny was born into that gang by blood since his older brothers were members. They put in a lot of work for the neighborhood. He had one brother who was in and out of prison, and the other was doing a long stretch upstate.

What people who aren't from the hood don't understand is that the hood is a jungle. It is as close as you can get to survival of the fittest in America. Weak people get taken advantage of. Bigger, more powerful gangs roll on smaller cliques, and all of this is painted on a canvas of life or death. The hand I was dealt, differed from the hand I chose to play, and it definitely differed from Johnny's. I had a loving family who were more than able to provide for me. I chose to get involved in tagging, drugs, and gangs. Johnny and I are examples of the two different reasons people get involved in gangs.

The first reason is you're conditioned into it. For example you might be into hip-hop, and over the years you keep hearing the same messages of selling drugs and shooting people and driving Mercedes. These messages are echoed in the neighborhood, shown to you by the extremely small percentage of gangsters who are actually living that lifestyle. Your parents can't even afford to put food on the table, but the local drug dealer is rolling around in a Mercedes S550 with 24-inch rims. This might condition you that this life is a cool thing.

The second reason is that you were born to a family who was gang banging. You see them doing it and you think that this is what life is supposed to be. That was Johnny's story. They broke the mold when they made Johnny. He was not physically imposing by any stretch, he was 5'8 and 160 pounds soaking wet, but he was always fighting. Either starting one, or finishing one. He was a warrior, and it showed on his face and in the way he walked – with his head and chin up, always on high alert, eyes scanning everyone and everything around him but in a calm way, like you didn't even know he was there. He just blended into the background, until he felt like it was time to make a move – real calculated like – then he would let all hell loose.

He was born into a street warrior's life just by being raised on that block. It was as natural as a Spartan born in Sparta. I never saw him back down from a fight – not once – and he was always the smaller guy. But he didn't care. He just loved to fight, and that's what we did. Hanging out on Johnny's block with Johnny meant you were going to get into a lot of violent fights. You had to be okay with that. If you held any shred of fear in your heart, you were on the wrong block, and it was best for everyone around if you left. Rival gangs would roll through our turf, and just as quick as they came, a melee involving twenty or thirty people would erupt in the middle of the street. Sometimes someone would blast off a couple rounds into the air, or into the crowd, and everyone would scatter before the police showed up. No one ever saw anything. I never did.

As I rolled through my seventeenth year, the gang rivalries escalated and the fights became more violent. I carried a weapon with me everywhere I went. Being caught by a rival gang without at least a knife to protect yourself was a death sentence. By this time, I was in and out of correctional facilities for so many offenses from graffiti to drug possession it would be tedious to list all of them. Whenever I got out, I wanted to do the two things I was deprived of in the joint – party and hook up with women.

On one such occasion, Johnny promised me a night of drugs and girls on my first night home, so I linked up with him as soon as I hit the street. We were hanging out drinking 707 malt liquor in my garage. Johnny said he knew a group of girls who were looking to kick it, and I pressed him to get them over.

The girls came through and we sat around drinking and shooting it back and forth. One of the girls, Jenny, was very flirty with me. We vibed throughout the night, and mostly kept to ourselves while the rest of the crowd did whatever it is they were doing. As it got later, I made it clear to Johnny that I wanted to get out of this scene and close the deal with her. I couldn't do it at my house because I had just gotten out of jail hours ago. I was not trying to give my mother trouble already, especially the kind of trouble that involves alcohol and women I don't know that well. He was not happy about my request to leave, but he agreed because when your friend gets out of jail, he's the homecoming king for the night. You have to make sure he gets fucked up and gets laid.

Johnny's house was only a few blocks away from mine so we decided to walk. It was late, about two in the morning, and the night would've ended much earlier if Johnny weren't trying, unsuccessfully, to hook up with Jenny's friend. We kicked everyone out of my garage and stumbled into the street. Johnny and I were messing around, pushing each other and laughing, reliving old times. He was happy I was out of jail, and we began making big plans for the future.

From behind, headlights lit us up like the field lights at Dodger Stadium. I froze as an accelerating engine screamed in our direction. The car blew through a stop sign, swerved around the three of us, and took off down the street. As the car shot by, the driver yelled something out of the window I could not understand.

"Yeah, fuck you too!" Johnny screamed back.

We weren't tripping. We just laughed the situation off as a typical two a.m. encounter. I followed the car's taillights with my eyes for a hundred yards. Then I saw the car pull a U-turn. It stopped ten yards from us. Time slowed as we stood blinded by the headlights, and the joking yielded to a serious energy.

Johnny said to me out of the side of his mouth, "If anyone steps out of this car, we're gonna fuck them up."

The passenger door opened and a man stepped out of the car. Without even saying a word, Johnny charged him. The gate raised – the bull was out. They began fighting in the middle of the street. I approached the car as the driver got out.

"Let's go, bro!" I screamed at the driver.

Since I was facing the headlights, all I could make out was the driver's silhouette. As he stepped out of the light I could see his full features, as well as the large handgun in his left hand. Time seemed to pause – then stretch and warp. My vision shook a little like it had just suffered an earthquake, and then all at once everything came back into focus as I stared down the barrel of his gun.

"This is my fucking hood," he snarled.

I thought maybe I had just woken up from a deep sleep like reality had shifted into a dream, but it did not. The only things that existed in that moment were him, the gun, and me. I thought about grabbing the barrel, but he could pull the trigger and that would be the end of me in a fraction of a second.

I was standing in front of the gun, and then I wasn't. It was that quick. Like I was plucked out of the dream, and placed back into reality. Johnny had pushed me out of the way and stepped in front of the gun.

"Why you pullin' guns out?" Johnny put his head against the barrel. "Pull the trigger. Pull the trigger. You're a fuckin' bitch if you don't pull that trigger!"

Johnny came on so aggressively that the guy holding the gun looked like he was the one on the defensive. All he could do was repeat, "Now you got a gun in your face!" The guy was full of shit. He would've pulled the trigger by then if he'd planned on shooting someone. We all knew that.

Johnny hit him with a right hook that sent him tumbling onto the pavement. The gun, and who ended up with it, was the only thing that mattered as they struggled for it in the street. I gave a wind up kick to the guy's head, which barely missed, grazing his forehead. I re-centered and aimed for another, when the passenger tackled me to the ground. The passenger and I were wrestling when a blast cut through the darkness. The smell of sulfur settled over us. We froze, looking to see what had happened.

The driver screamed, "Let's go, let's go!" The guys ran to the car, and sped off.

My ears were ringing from the gunshot. The wail of their car accelerating to a high speed and Jenny's screams of, "Oh my God, they killed him! He's dead!" were coming in and out in muffled bursts. I was slightly disoriented. Then I saw Johnny's body lying in the street. He was lying on his side, his back to me. I walked over to him expecting the worst. I already had an image in my head of what I was going to see. Then he rolled over.

"Shit! He's alive. Are you hit?"

He got on his hands and knees and looked up at the streetlight. "Fuck. That was loud."

"Are you hit?"

He patted his chest, abdomen, and upper thighs.

"Nah, I'm good."

He picked his head up and the streetlight illuminated his face. The tip of his nose and his lips were black with gunpowder burns. I grabbed his head gently and turned it. He had a wound from a bullet graze. It looked a little deeper than a scratch, and it ran from his lip to his ear. The driver tried to shoot Johnny in the face. At the same time he pulled the trigger, Johnny hit his arm upward causing the bullet to graze. A half-second later, or a millimeter to the right, and Johnny's head would have been blown off.

The three of us collected ourselves and went home that night. Later that month we found out who the driver was. We got our payback, and never spoke of it again. Every action done to us, created an equal or greater reaction from us. It's the physics of the streets.

***

Gang fights, shootings, stabbings – it all became part of daily life. I thought there was nothing unusual about it. We would hang on the block or stand on the street corner and a car would drive by and fire shots into our crowd.

What I have learned through my journey is that the gang life is bullshit. You commit crimes, follow orders, and put yourself in harm's way for the benefit of someone higher than you on the food chain. That person doesn't care about you or your family; they just want to make money off you. They sell you the idea of an ultimate bond and a loyalty to your crew. But that is a romanticized story. It isn't reality.

You are sold on the idea that it is glamorous. Society's conditioning and portrayal of what a gangster is, is appealing. In the movies, these guys are buying off lawyers and judges and importing Central American cocaine by the planeload. Kids see that and think they are going to be the biggest baller on the block. They think they are going to be that guy they saw in the movies. Then they go into it, and it may be fun and glamorous in the beginning, but the reality of it is pain, loneliness, jail time, and death. There are people who want to kill you simply because of the block you live on. And people around you are getting killed all the time. There was a shooting yesterday, and last week; or the house next to yours gets shot up.

I happened by chance to go through a situation that validated the ride or die loyalty of gang life. Johnny pushed me out of the way of that gun and took a bullet for me. I thought the loyalty, brotherhood, and willingness to die for one another was real. I knew the possibility of being killed any random night was also real. It was a tradeoff I was willing to make. I was committed after that. I believed in the game.

The lifestyle is fast and dangerous. I thought I was one step away from donning a suit, walking into the back of restaurants, and eating for free like Ray Liotta and Joe Pesce in "Goodfellas." In reality, I was climbing the wrong way on the ladder, descending into the black abyss of violence, drugs, and crime, which few pull themselves out of.

The stress of that life creates a state of pure insanity. The only way for me to deal with it was drugs. While I was in that convoluted, drug-fueled mindset, the stress and insanity began to seem appealing.

***

It was the night I let the beast that was always inside me – sleeping but present – out of the cage.

We were hanging around smoking and drinking. The night was dull, and I was fading in and out of sleep. I nodded out for a moment and woke up to reach for a beer. Christy was sitting on the couch, looking anxiously at the phone on the table.

"What are you doing?" I said.

"I'm waiting for the drop-off," she replied.

A shipment of drugs was coming in, and it was her job to pick it up and cut it into smaller portions for street level selling. I assumed this meant cocaine, and was excited that she chose me to help her with the task. It meant that I would have access to all the free cocaine I wanted as we took up the task of cutting it and packaging it.

Dusk turned into night, then midnight, as we waited for her man to come by with the shipment. The first rule in the drug game is the dealer is always late. Impatience is a useless reaction and gets you on the wrong side of everyone's nerves. I ran out of my personal supply and was nodding in and out of consciousness from the combination of weed and liquor.

Finally he arrived, and quite frankly I was a little irritated at having to wait so long. Real gangsters shouldn't have to wait that long. Michael Corleone never waited. He made people wait. How dare I be forced to wait? I stayed inside and smoked a cigarette while Christy did the deal.

She came barreling through the door in a full sprint and tossed three sandwich bags of drugs on the coffee table. She couldn't sit down fast enough to cut the bag open with her pocketknife. She poured me a small amount of the drugs onto a CD case on the coffee table next to the ashtray, which had my half-smoked cigarette sticking out of it.

Something was way off. It should've been powder, but it looked like shards of glass. It was meth. She crushed the glass into powder, which she pushed into a small pile that she snorted. I desperately wished I had more willpower to either play it cool or get up and leave. I really wanted to be in touch with those emotions. But I was so far from that place. I was neck deep in self-destruction, ravaged by a crack cocaine habit and desensitized to crime and violence on levels most people will never experience. I didn't care about anything anymore. My life, my family, and their well-being were the farthest things from my mind. Deep down in the core of my soul, I knew I had let them, and myself, down. I chose the path, and I was going to walk down it until I walked into a life sentence or the grave.

Christy and I stayed up all night smoking meth. It just clicked with me, like finding your favorite flavor of ice cream. All the other flavors were good, but when I found this flavor, nothing could compare. Part of me believes my lifelong Ritalin prescription primed me for my love affair with meth. They are essentially the same drug, and I had been prescribed Ritalin since I was seven years old. But that's a useless theory at this point. Back to the story:

I went home after the all night bender with Christy, and ran into my mother. The sun had already been up for a few hours. She had become accustomed to seeing me come home at all odd hours of the morning, and knew that her words and warnings were futile. She resigned herself to firing me looks of disgust and disappointment that echoed louder in my head than any lecture she gave me.

Meth had a much more insidious pull over me than crack cocaine did. Everyone I know who has ever had a problem with meth says some variation of "the drug takes your soul." Relationships with people – family, friends, and lovers – are put to the side. They mean nothing. The drug is in control and you are completely willing to watch your soul get sucked right through that pipe.

Everyone has their tweak – a tick or hobby – they like to do while they are high on meth. Some people will smoke a bowl and work on their car for ten straight hours. Others will clean their houses all day and night. My tweak was stealing shit. At the time, it was an effective tweak. It satisfied the compulsive aspect of the meth high and allowed me to get money to fund my habit. But everyone has to pay the piper eventually. The financial, emotional, and spiritual price of meth is steep. I began stealing anything and everything from anyone and everyone, especially my family.

I was racking up drug debts to dangerous people and received phone calls at all hours of the night from dealers threatening to kill me. But I knew they were bluffing. You can't kill someone who owes you money – there's no one to collect from. But I knew they weren't above torturing me or coming after my family. It was grim. I would steal from one person to pay a dealer back, only to end up in debt to another before the day was over.

Meth is a powerful stimulant that keeps you awake, sometimes for days at a time. It is pleasurable at first, but by day three you end up borderline psychotic, and you get sloppy. Not good for someone who makes their living in a high stakes, fast paced business like crime. I was careless with my robberies and paid the price by going in and out of jail for parole violations, petty thefts, and other low-level druggie offenses. My rap sheet soon printed out like a receipt from the grocery store.

My family wrote me off at this point and for good cause. I couldn't be trusted. Aunts and uncles hid their wallets and purses at family functions, and I could sense their unease when I came around. That was hard for me. I was close with my family. When they didn't want to be around me anymore, I knew it was getting bad.

My cousin Freddy wasn't ready to disown me just yet. Coming from a place of calm understanding, he would drop little lines of simple wisdom that gave me hope. He used to say to me, "Just chill out, ya know. Have a couple of beers and watch the game. There's no need to get all crazy. Just stay away from the hard stuff, man." I nodded in willfully ignorant agreement that maybe I could just have a couple beers and watch the game. I didn't need the hard stuff; a life of crime wasn't for me. I just had to grow up and stop acting out. All I wanted was everything to be normal again.

Freddy was always cool towards me and gave me a lot more leeway than I deserved. I really did appreciate all that he did for me. He was one of the last people left in my life, and I was desperately trying not to burn this final bridge. I would kick it with him, but was careful not to stay too long or show up too frequently. I did not want to wear out my welcome with him. But it was only a matter of time before I let him down, as well.

My mother was the cleaner of the family; she'd clean everyone's house. She loved cleaning so much that my father bought her a gold broom pendant one year for their anniversary. She had a set of keys to everyone's house. She would clean their place during the day while they were at work.

As drug addicts, we always hurt the people that are closest to us. Freddy was one of the only people still hanging out with me, trying to set me straight. He still trusted me, however little that was, and that trust was there for me to exploit. Addicts are like that in active addiction. Everyone becomes a means to an end – a tool to utilize when needed. It is not out of malice, but rather an extreme selfishness and desperation.

I was kicked out of my house during this time so I broke in during the middle of the day when I knew my parents were running errands. I snuck in through the garage, like I had done a thousand times before, and took the keys to Freddy's house.

The plan was to break into his house while he worked the day shift at Von's supermarket. It would be quick and easy. I was going to make off with just enough to get my fix for the next few days, then return the keys to my mother's house before anyone found out. I soon discovered one small problem.

Von's employees were on a nationwide strike so Freddy and his girl weren't working. I was jonesin' for a fix, and these details were getting in the way of what I had to do. My best thinking told me to hastily break into their house in the middle of the night. I was in the worst possible condition I could have been in - coming down off a meth run.

I entered the front door and tiptoed around looking for his wallet or her purse. I couldn't find either on the first floor. The wallets had to be in their room. I cursed under my breath because I knew they were both upstairs sleeping. My body was hurting and aching from withdrawal. As much I did not want to, I was going into that bedroom.

I crept up the stairs, whispering to myself how stupid this idea was. I crisscrossed the staircase on the tips of my toes, trying to be as quiet as I could. I was a neurotic, sweating mess.

I cracked the door open. They were sound asleep. I scanned the room and saw her purse lying next to the bed. I slowly lowered myself to a crouch and crawled on my knees and elbows across the floor until I reached the purse. As I grabbed it, I heard --

"Freddy, hey Freddy. I think someone is in the house," she whispered as she shook him awake.

I tucked into a fetal position at the foot of the bed, and stayed as quiet as possible. A million different thoughts of how I was going to get myself out of this one ran through my mind.

"Go check it out," she urged him.

He got out of bed and saw me right away.

"Hey, Chris. What are you doing here, bro?" He looked concerned but also suspicious. I was relieved that he didn't look angry, but this was bad. There was no explaining my way out of this one.

"Can I crash here, man? I haven't been doing so good." I said, hopelessly.

"Yeah, of course. You can take the couch downstairs. But what the fuck are you doing in my room?"

The girlfriend got up, grabbed her purse and put it in the drawer of the nightstand. She knew I had problems, but I think she doubted I would do something as brazenly crazy as try to rob her purse next to the bed she was sleeping in.

I walked out of the room a completely bankrupt and defeated man. As I walked down the stairs, I heard the door to his room lock behind me. With that click, the last person holding out hope for me shut me out of his life. I was alone. I had burned the last bridge.

Word quickly got around to the rest of the family. My mom and dad were the only people who would still take my phone call, but they would not let me stay at their house. I went to live on Johnny's couch.

I always stayed at Johnny's when I got kicked out of my house. His mom would let us stay there, despite knowing we were using and selling drugs. His mom was dealing with a lot. Johnny's older brother was doing a long bid in prison and his other brothers were gone to the streets. She felt like she lost her boys, and Johnny being the youngest, she tried to keep him as close as possible. I guess she figured it was better to have us under her roof where we were safe. That became my main place to go.

She showed me compassion during a time in my life when few others did. She knew I was in and out of prison, knew I was on drugs, and knew I was always on the run from somebody, but she let me stay on her couch anyway. She wasn't a mother figure to me, but she showed me the depth of compassion a mother possesses. I tried to give her money or groceries whenever I could.

***

Most of my cousins are around the same age as me. Growing up we did everything together. Frequent family functions - barbecues, birthday parties, holiday gatherings - created a close bond between all of us. When everyone wrote me off, it hurt. My heart ached, but I knew I deserved it. Still, I had to push those emotions away, or be consumed by them.

Shortly after the debacle at Freddy's house, I was riding my bike down the block where my cousin Rich lives next door to Freddy. When he saw me riding by, he waved me down. I had a moment of excitement that one of my cousins wanted to speak to me. I didn't even care what he wanted to talk about.

That excitement quickly vanished when he started questioning me. He heard about what happened and wanted to know what was up with me. I could sense he was trying to feel me out, but did so in a subtle way as not to alarm me.

He didn't come right out and say it, but he was implying that I shouldn't come around. He didn't trust me. If I could rob Freddy, if I could sink so deep that I would rob my own family, I was capable of anything.

Even though I was breaking her heart, mom was always there for me, even when I went to prison. She'd tell me that I could still fix this, that I could still fix myself. She kept alive a faint glimmer of living hope when all I saw was black. But I was far from living at this point. I just existed. My world was getting smaller by the day. I woke up, hustled enough money to get my fix, and got as high as I could until the day turned into night, into day again, and repeated. On the horizon there were only dark clouds and storms.

I turned eighteen while on probation. The probation dance meant checking in with my probation officer, keeping him updated on my current residence, and showing up for drug tests. Mentally I was out to lunch while using meth. Things like checking in with my P.O. went from priorities to long lost suggestions. I didn't even have a permanent residence. Soon I stopped showing up for my routine appointments with my P.O. and drug counselor. As the Los Angeles County Department of Corrections put it, I was "on the run."

I was making a measly living as a burglar of all specialties – houses, cars, and businesses. The beginning of the end of this run was robbing a K-Mart. After I got busted, the police saw that I had an outstanding arrest warrant for the parole violations, and I expected to be thrown in jail right there. But they gave me a court date and let me go on my own recognizance.

Three days later, I was shoving a lock-picking kit in my pants at an Auto Zone in San Pedro. I walked out and saw a car coming right for me.

"Huh, that's weird, I wonder if this guy is going to stop," I thought.

"Okay, he's definitely not going to stop. Shit, they're trying to run up on me!"

I was sure it was a rival gang coming for me. My time had finally come. I braced for a fight. I was going to take as many of them out with me as I could.

"What's up, fool! Let's go! Do something!" I shouted at the car.

Two guys, dressed in normal clothes and tatted up like I was, leapt from the sedan. They pulled out .9 mm Glocks. I waited for the sound of gunshots, and the stabbing, burning sensation of bullets entering my body.

"L.A.P.D! Get the fuck on the ground!" I was equally as relieved as I was pissed off. Like a ragdoll, physically and emotionally, I dropped to my knees with my hands on my head.

They didn't let me go this time. I would spend the next twenty months in county jail and then prison. I wish I had a better story for how my time on the run ended, maybe a midnight car chase through the streets, or holed up in a house with a SWAT team outside. But no, it was petty thefts and parole violations. It's not the big crime that gets a gangster popped. It's the little ones, the ones that are supposed to be easy. So easy that gangsters get careless. The pebbles trip us up, then the boulders loosen, and then the whole hillside comes crashing down, settling in the same spots for every gangster – the penitentiary or the grave.

Chapter Four

I sat in a holding cell at the downtown Los Angeles police station waiting to see a judge.

On meth life speeds up, and when you come down from the high, it crashes to a halt. The realization of what you've done and the emotions you have been running from catch up and flood in, like waves rolling on to the shore. The memories of crimes, the people I had hurt and stolen from, all rushed into my consciousness at once. Guilt and shame washed over me. I didn't sleep for two days in the holding cell. On the third day, I went before the judge.

He set a court date – a routine procedure – and I went back to the holding cell where I waited for the sheriff's deputies to take me to the county jail.

As I sat there in the pain and despair of my comedown, across the cell I saw an older inmate who had "San Pedro" tattooed across his arm. I felt like a soldier missing in action who stumbled upon a unit with his own country's flag stitched on the uniform. I got to talking to him, and we asked each other about people we knew in common. He mentioned two names. I did know them. In fact, I was close with them. They were his kids.

He took a liking to me after that, and told me he would look after me. I was grateful because I knew I was going to prison, and I had never done the real deal before.

I had spent a lot of time in juvenile detention centers and camps, but I had never gone to county jail or state prison. I had heard about it. One of my homies had an older brother who went away, and one of the guys on the block did time. But I figured the stories I had heard were exaggerated to inflate the ego of whoever was telling them.

Other guys told me stories of indiscriminate stabbings and murders by guys who would snap, either from the stress of solitary confinement while in the hole, or from the sheer psychological strain of prison itself. There were other stories, most of them made up by older homies who wanted to scare us younger guys. I had no idea what to expect, and the fear of the unknown made me anxious and unsettled. No matter which stories were true or false, I knew there was going to be violence.

That didn't scare me. What scared me was the unpredictability of the situation. I was entering a dark corner of reality that exists entirely separate from the free world. There are rules and laws that govern the prison world that I did not know. It caused an underlying tension in me, a constant anxiety trying to predict the impending violence.

As the old man and I played cards while we waited for the bus to take us to county, he gave me a crash course on the do's-and-don'ts of prison. He kept repeating one line. He could not get off it, as if it were welded into his psyche from years of experience.

"Don't fuck with the cops."

We would play a hand of cards, he would rattle off some quick tips, freeze and look me straight in the eye, pause, then say "and do not fuck with the cops."

"It's not like the streets. The cops don't have any rules in here. They are king, and they will fuck you up. You do not...fuck with the cops."

"Time to go. Let's move, up and out." The deputy sheriff ordered us onto the bus to county jail, which at the time was a complete clusterfuck of an operation.

Sheriff Lee Baca was in charge of the county jail system when I was doing time there in 2005 to 2006. Since then, he has been convicted of federal charges of conspiracy, obstruction of justice, and giving false statements relating to a conspiracy scandal involving inmate abuse.

Reading that in the paper as I sat down for breakfast with my wife – pregnant with our first child, I couldn't help but laugh. I can confirm those charges. The L.A. county jail system wasn't fit for animals, let alone humans.

Arriving at the jail, we were herded off the bus like cattle. I was chained to the old man, and we marched through the doors of the downtown Los Angeles jail – the Twin Towers. As we shuffled our way through the main intake door, he turned and whispered one last time, "Hey. Don't fuck with the cops!" I wasn't sure what was coming next, but I had one rock solid piece of advice to work with.

The intake process was long, and the county jail was so overcrowded that we had to wait four days just to get a bed. The "bed" would almost certainly be on the floor of a cell because they were sleeping five men to a four-man cell at the time. The fifth man was – unfortunately for him - the "floor sleeper."

The sheriffs led us to a corridor, which had a yellow square and a red square painted next to each other in the middle of the floor. "Stand in the yellow box, throw your clothes in the red box! Anyone causing trouble or holding things up will go back to the beginning of the intake process!" barked a deputy.

Every one of the deputies in county looked like they were on a heavy dose of steroids. They were the meanest looking cops you would ever hope not to see. Part of the routine process of becoming an L.A. County sheriff's deputy is a stint working in the county jail. Most deputies serve a couple of months and then go on regular patrol at an assigned station. But some cops, usually the sickest, meanest motherfuckers, choose to stay at county jail permanently. In their own hopeless way, they become as warped as the inmates.

We stood naked in a circle while deputies searched our clothes. A guy across the way from me bent down and rested his hands on his knees. It seemed harmless enough, but a deputy pulled him up by the shoulder and hit him hard in the stomach. The man keeled over and hit the floor. Two other cops dragged him away by his arms like they were taking out the trash.

I knew then that the old man was spot on with his –"don't fuck with the cops" advice. He was standing next to me, and I expected him to lean over and give me his usual line, but he said "Eyes and ears open, mouth shut. Even if you know what's going on, you don't gotta tell anyone." After the intake process, I was separated from the old man. The large group I came in with was split up and shuffled from cell to overcrowded cell while we waited for beds to open.

There were up to forty guys sleeping in a sixteen-person holding cell. It was mayhem, and the overcrowding led to daily fights. The heat or the stress would get to a guy, he would find something wrong with someone else, and there would be a fight. The seasoned gang guys had been through this before and knew to keep to themselves. This was just a circus for them, a sideshow. They were waiting to get on the cell block where they could link up with their crews and get on with business.

I would have a gang to run with, as well. I ran with a Mexican gang on the streets, and in prison all Mexican gangs run with the Southsiders. Some guys had told me I would have a hard time running with the Southsiders in prison because my skin was so white, but I was counting on my street affiliation to counter my skin color.

Other gangs consolidate under their own flag, and everything is divided along racial lines. Mexicans, Blacks, and Whites all have their own organizations, which have subsets based on what gang they were affiliated with on the streets. No one runs without a gang in prison. If you aren't affiliated with a gang on the street, you quickly find one once you get to prison. Run without a gang and you're a man without a country –a target for exploitation, extortion, or worse.

After a few days I got my cell assignment – C block cell three. They marched a bunch of us in a single file line to C wing. The guy in front of me was supposed to be in cell four, but his roommate turned out to be a rival gang member. When the roommate found out the new guy's gang affiliation, he pulled out an eight-inch knife that looked like it came out of a "Rambo" movie, and threatened to cut him up if he came into the cell. The guy chose to go to the hole instead. During all this, I kept my eyes locked on the wall. You can get stabbed just for being nosy.

What stood out to me most, as I walked through the cellblock corridor, was the presence of bars. They were oppressive and disinterested – they didn't care who you were, what your crime was, what gang you were affiliated with, or what race you were. The steel was cold and hard, and treated everyone the same. The bars also struck me with a sense of permanence that had never dawned on me before I saw them. I could intellectualize the concept of being locked up, my freedom taken from me, but when I saw the bars it became real. The realization dawned on me that I was about to be locked in a cage for a significant amount of time.

I entered my cell in the middle of the night and saw all the beds were filled. I stood there awkwardly, holding my belongings – my toiletries and an extra pair of county blues – and waited for something to happen.

One of the homies on the bottom right bunk woke up and took a look at me. "What up, wood?" he said.

Wood is short for "peckerwood," prison slang for a white person. I am fair skinned, and this furthered my anxiety that I would be too white to run with the Mexicans in jail. But I wasn't white enough to run with the Caucasian gangs either. My stomach began twisting and turning.

"I'm not a wood, I'm a homie," I said hesitantly. A homie is slang for a fellow Mexican gang member.

He was lying on his shoulder. He cocked his head, and squinted to get a better look at me. After looking me up and down, he turned to the bunkmate across from him and barked at him in Spanish. The man in the bunk got up without a word and pulled a mattress out from under the bunk. He gave his bunk up to me, but not by choice. I was a Southsider – he was not. I outranked him.

I inwardly sighed with relief at navigating the first hurdle of my prison career. I had a gang and I would be protected. I was still nervous and fearful, but at least I had a crew and wasn't a sitting duck waiting to be robbed or stabbed as an initiation for some punk kid trying to earn his stripes.

I stayed in county jail for four months before I was sent to state prison. I lived in the same cell for that time without a problem except the one time I fought my British cellmate. I didn't fight him by choice; I had to do it because of a racial conflict between the Mexicans and Whites. A fight broke out between a Mexican who had just received a life sentence and a White who was talking shit that the new lifer was in no mood to hear. The argument escalated to threats, and I knew a riot was coming.

My new British cellmate was massive – 6'4," 250 pounds, in his mid thirties. I was 5'5", 150 pounds, and eighteen. I was shaking at the thought of being stuck in a cage, engaged in hand-to-hand combat with this brute; but what my gang would do to me for defying orders was much worse.

Around 1 p.m., a Southsider whose job was to clean the tier, came around with a mop and bucket and told all the Southsiders that a riot with the Whites was to go down at the 7 p.m. pill call. I was so nervous my hands started to shake. I looked around for something I could make a weapon from, like in prison television shows. Nothing came to hand.

Not even an hour later the same Southsider rolls by with his mop and bucket again. He leaned into each cell with a Southsider in it and gave a message.

When he got to my cell, I found out what the message was: "We aren't going to be able to open all the cells for a riot. So if you have access to a White then you have a green light." In other words, I had the order to engage them in combat and kill if necessary. I nodded and stared at the floor. I didn't have just any White guy in my cell. I had this massive brute and it was obvious who was going to come out on top.

I had to get him while he was still sleeping, which he'd been doing most of the afternoon. I looked down at him and carefully planned how I was going to pull this off. I didn't have any room for mistakes or half measures – I had to go 100 mph right out of the starting gate. I got ready to make a move, then got nervous, and began pacing around the cell.

I finally got my nerve back and looked down my target - the left side of his head was exposed as he was sleeping on his right shoulder. I cocked back and hit him as hard as I could right in the temple. I hit him with every ounce of strength. All my aggression was packed into this one punch.

He wheeled out of the bunk. My knees weakened. I thought I was going to pass out. I'd just hit him with the best shot I'd ever hit anyone with in my life, and this guy stood up like he brushed off a mosquito.

I stuttered and mumbled trying to explain. "The-, th-, th-, they said..."was all I could get out.

He rushed me and crashed into me like a linebacker with his shoulder and elbow. I went flying into the bars behind me. It felt like I was airborne for minutes. I recovered, rushed him back, and swung wildly like a trapped animal that knew its last moments were approaching.

He let me wear myself out, deflecting my punches with ease, and throwing several blows that hit me like slabs of concrete. When it was over, we both sat on our bunks adjacent from one another huffing and puffing.

"You did what you had to do. We cool?" he said. My ego wouldn't allow me to be the one to extend the olive branch, but I was relieved when he did.

"Yeah, we're cool," I replied.

When a prison riot takes place people get injured, others get time added to their sentence, and whoever started it has to explain themselves to the gang leaders. I did not need to get caught up in that drama. Instead, we agreed to sweep our scuffle under the rug in the interest of keeping things smooth between the Whites and the Mexicans.

The Brit bought some food from the commissary and shared it with me in a gesture of peace, in a "I break bread with you" sort of way. He was in jail for a DUI, in which he was caught with 350 rounds of armor piercing bullets. He wasn't a bad guy or even dangerous. He was just a redneck type. He could've killed me the day we got into a scuffle, but he showed me mercy. We became really close over the next few months before I headed off to prison. He taught me a lot about life, like a big brother.

***

I was assigned to Delano state prison and served sixteen months there, on top of the four I'd done in county. When I got out, I made a pact with myself that I would never go back. I would quit hard drugs and alcohol and stay out of the streets. I would never put my family through an ordeal like that again. I'd clean up my act and get a regular job just like any other average Joe.

Chapter Five

I was out of prison a total of nineteen days. Within the first week, I ended up strung out on meth, homeless, suicidal, and worse off than before I got locked up. My first mistake was having my ex-girlfriend Kim pick me up upon my release.

My sister Toni introduced us, way back in the day, but she came to dislike Kim. Kim was just as wild and wrapped up in the street life as I was. We had a volatile, drug-fueled relationship before I went away, and when I got out, we picked up right where we left off. I was using drugs with her on the car ride home and that was that – like I never stopped at all.

When I got back to the neighborhood, I expected to be greeted with a welcome home party like a soldier coming back from a tour of duty. I was supposed to be the Viking walking into Valhalla. That could not have been farther from the reality. When you're in prison, time stops. You are counting the days until you can get back to life as you know it, but life as you know it doesn't exist anymore. While you're locked up – standing still in time – the outside world is carrying on. When I went back to my block, I was forgotten. I was a ghost. A couple of people showed me love and gave me free drugs out of courtesy, but the overwhelming majority could not have cared less.

My parents were heartbroken when they saw me getting loaded again. I could see it in my mother's eyes when she saw me high. She had to kick me out of the house. As I walked out the door, she said words that would haunt me – "We stayed by you and look what happened again." I didn't have a response. No response would have been adequate. I nodded, turned around, and went to the car where my dad was waiting to drop me off at Johnny's house.

The car ride was silent, and the atmosphere so heavy it held me down in the seat. I almost choked on the tension. I couldn't turn to face my dad. I stared blankly out the window, watching normal people carry on with their day. I looked at their faces and the humanity that I had lost. I would have switched places with any one of them. My mindset was a hopeless acceptance of the fact that this is who I was, and who I was going to be, for the rest of my life.

We arrived at Johnny's house and I took my belongings out of the car. All I possessed at the time were the clothes I had on my back, plus some extra socks and underwear. It was consolidated into a drawstring backpack with a broken string. I didn't say anything to my father and sheepishly walked up Johnny's front steps. I could hear the car pull away in the background. I knocked on Johnny's door three times and waited. Nothing. I knocked again and waited. Still no answer.

Of course, he wouldn't be home. Everything that could go wrong, went wrong. To make matters worse, I was crashing hard from my last meth run and was running into walls of fatigue and depression. I had nowhere to go. I scanned the street for a place to figure out my next move and saw the San Pedro Library across the way. I had enough energy to make it to the front steps, where I collapsed and lit a cigarette.

I was completely exhausted, worn out from life. The fight to hustle was gone from me. I slouched against the library's cold marble façade, feeling the full force of the comedown, and nodded off. Then a thought rocketed into my consciousness like a missile. It jarred me awake with a shot of adrenaline – I am homeless. I am sleeping on the steps of a library like a bum. Because I am a bum! I have no home, no car, no respect. I have nothing.

Kim had disappeared days ago. God only knew where she was or what drugs she was on.

My face tightened into a grimace as I digested the sour reality my brain bit into. I shook my head, flicked my cigarette into the gutter, and made my decision. I was done. I had ridden this train to the end of the line. There was nowhere else to go, no future for me.

Over the next week I hustled enough money to get the minimum fix I needed to stay well and saved the rest of the cash to buy a gun. I was sleeping outside under storefront awnings and highway underpasses. One of my homies sold me a .9 mm Smith and Wesson. I got it on the cheap, probably because it was a hot gun - it had been used in a crime and was being passed off – but I didn't care. I wasn't going to be around much longer.

The depth and weight of suicide became real after I bought the gun. I looked over its black metal and thought about how hard it would be for my parents. They would be devastated, but I rationalized that it was like ripping off a Band-Aid – it would hurt at first, but it would hurt a lot less than tearing it off slowly. Eventually life would go on for them.

I thought it over for a moment and then realized I couldn't take my own life. I just didn't have it in me to go out by own hand. I decided that suicide by cop was a better choice. I had the perfect plan for how I'd do it.

While I was incarcerated, I learned the rules and classifications of criminals in the prison hierarchy. At the very bottom of this totem pole are child molesters. This sparked the idea of simultaneously cleaning up San Pedro and committing suicide by cop. I was going to locate all of the local child molesters through the sex offender registry. Then I would show up at their front door and shoot them in the face as soon as they answered. I figured I would kill a handful before word got around. The cops would be called, and it would end in a shootout. In my drug crazed, suicidal state, this seemed like a sound idea. It satisfied me, but I couldn't go through with it.

San Pedro is small, and everyone knows each other. The Luera name is well-known and has a good reputation. My father worked on the docks for over fifty years; my cousins and uncles were all accomplished athletes at San Pedro High School. If I went through with this plan, the name would be forever tarnished. I was already giving the Luera name a bad rep with the life I was leading. I didn't have to totally blow it up through my death.

I couldn't even make the decision to die. I did the next best thing that I thought of for my family and that was push them away. I stopped trying with them, figuring they were better off without me in their lives. The ones that wouldn't let go, I made them let go. I didn't want to drag them anymore. I fell off the radar. I went dark.

The remainder of those nineteen days I spent stealing cars to chop, and breaking into cars for valuables. My crime spree was relentless – nearly around the clock – it was only a matter of when, not if, I was going to get caught. I was popped trying to steal a Ford Expedition.

I was back upstate in prison, and it was the same deal I had been doing since I was twelve years old, but with more baggage. First off, my addiction was out of control. Before I left for prison I had a $200 per day habit. The car thefts yielded me plenty of money, and every last dime went to getting high. Second, I went up to prison still dating Kim. We fed off each other and many of my relapses upon release from detention centers, camps, and finally prison were with Kim. She liked to do pills, which I would never touch because my birth mother overdosed on them. So Kim would do her pills and nod off, and I'd smoke my speed and start another run. We were as toxic as could be for one another, but good luck trying to tell that to two people who are in the thick of their addictions.

When you are in prison, you take a hiatus from reality. You live in this box that exists separately from the outside world. The violence and danger of that environment requires that you keep your head screwed on tight and you always remain sharp. You have to push out of your consciousness every possible emotion that could distract you. You have to realize the reality of the seriousness of the world you are in. The last thing I needed was to be worrying about a girl who was running around on the street. I stuffed any emotions I had for her, as well as the guilt, remorse, and self-loathing, down, and eventually out of my mind.

I told Kim before I left that she needed to do her thing while I was away. I was under no illusion that she was going to stay faithful to me for the two years I'd be gone. I didn't want to deal with the emotional hangup after she inevitably found someone else. I told her to do whatever she wanted – just stay by me mentally and write me letters. Mail is a huge thing in jail; it is the headliner of the day. When mail call is run, everyone waits quietly as the guards announce who received a letter or package. Everyone wants mail. It is the only connection to the outside world and the only interaction with real, free people. I wanted Kim to write me letters to keep me connected to the outside – a string to tether me to reality. Before I left I said I had two rules: "Don't mess around with your ex-boyfriend, and don't get pregnant." Simple, I thought.

The first year of my sentence went as well as I could have hoped for. I was writing Kim, my parents, and my biological sister Danielle on a consistent basis. That's when I found out all of the information on my biological mother. I got pretty close to Danielle; her letters came like clockwork. I could bet on my commissary that I would get a letter from Danielle to the day that it came.

My sister Toni would come up to visit, bringing with her whoever could make it up that weekend. Their support kept me in good spirits. Then with around eight months left in my sentence Kim went MIA. She didn't come to visit anymore, and the letters stopped coming, as well. I got one or two random letters before I was released – I knew something was up. Maybe she found someone else, which was to be expected. I wasn't tripping on that.

Danielle picked me up when I got out. She drove me back to her house in Bakersfield, where my mother and Toni picked me up. The ride back was awkward. I could tell Toni knew something she didn't want to tell me, and I had a suspicion it had to do with Kim.

"Anybody seen Kim lately?" I asked.

Toni hesitantly replied, "Oh, um...you didn't hear the news? She and Sammy (her ex) are going to have another baby."

I couldn't help but laugh. That's just the way things go when you are locked up. The outside world keeps turning and you are stuck.

***

When I got out, I had no plan to change. I hoped for the best, but by day three or four, I quickly found myself caught in that horrific mental state of staring down the forked path and knowing I was going to go back into the woods. Once I started drinking and using drugs, I lost all control. I was back to my old habits, habits that my parents were beyond fed up with.

They kicked me out of the house within the first week and I was back on the streets, staying with women, or sleeping in trap houses just to have a place to stay. Whenever I was staying at a house I always tried to make sure the fridge was stocked. It was how I established myself in their household. If the mother drank wine I stole a few bottles from Von's to give to her. If I was staying in a drug house, I hooked the owner up with free drugs and used their place as a homebase for selling. I knew how to get by. It was all a game and everyone wants something. If you find out what that is and give it to them, you'll be amazed at the slack people will cut you. Then I linked up with the chop racket again and kept them in a steady supply of stolen cars. I had a place to stay and a stream of income – I had all the fuel I needed.

Things were darker and colder now. I was older and had two prison terms under my belt. I wasn't just a bad kid getting into some mischief – I was a criminal, drug addict, and gang member. I was making an important and dangerous transition in my life. I wasn't committing crimes and living this lifestyle for the thrill of it anymore. It became who I was, my identity, and my sense of self.

I was more brazen and cunning than ever before. I assembled a crew to commit home invasions and steal cars with. We would break into houses and cars in broad daylight. I walked around with a chrome .45 Smith & Wesson handgun on me everywhere I went because I was convinced I was going to be killed at any moment – either by the cops or by a rival gang. It was a time of no rules, of anything goes. The chaos was constant. It was around the clock insanity. If I didn't get killed, I was definitely going back to prison. I knew it wouldn't be long until one of those options came true. That day came when I got caught stealing a Denali in Palos Verdes.

I should have known better than to go messing around in Palos Verdes. It is an affluent part of town and anything that looks out of the ordinary calls for an entire squadron of police to show up.

I had rolled up there with another guy in a stolen car looking for an easy target one night. We found one, in a garage that was left open. That's what kind of neighborhood it was – the kind where people leave their garage doors open at night. You can imagine what kind of police force comes with towns like this —white, armed to the teeth, and no tolerance for any shit like two guys rolling around in a stolen car, looking for another car to steal.

I got out to look in the garage, and my buddy went to ditch the stolen car. Before I got out, I took the .45 off my ankle and left it in the glove box. I was annoyed that it was so heavy. It made walking difficult. This would prove to be a crucial move – had I been caught with the .45 I would still be sitting in prison today.

I opened the Denali's door, which was unlocked, and hopped into a beautiful black vehicle with twenty-two inch low profile wheels. I found a set of keys in an unlocked glove box. The engine fired up with a growl, and then idled in a deep, strong hum. Elation came over me followed by a sense of urgency to get out of there as fast as I could.

Palos Verdes sits on top of a large hill overlooking the ocean. The streets are winding labyrinths that snake through the mountain. I was trying to navigate my way down the hill but my unfamiliarity with the area and my intoxication made it difficult to find my way. I had been drinking all night and smoking meth for several days. I was in a thick mental fog, and although my memory of that night is still hazy to this day, I assume I was lost and driving around in circles. A neighbor saw this and called the cops. I turned down a side street, not realizing it was a cul-de-sac. At the end of that cul-de-sac, a patrol car and two cops were standing next to the first stolen car my accomplice had ditched earlier.

They were writing a report and didn't see me, so I played it cool, slowly reversing the car out of the street. Just as I was pulling out of the cul-de-sac, one cop tapped his partner in the chest and pointed to me. They jumped in their car and came after me. I panicked and reversed down the street, accelerating quickly to a high rate of speed. I reached about forty miles per hour when I jack-knifed the Denali into a row of parked cars.

I dashed out of the truck and began running through backyards. I had no idea where I was going, but I knew Palos Verdes was a big hill so I kept running down. It had not even been a full minute since the police saw me in the cul-de-sac, sirens were coming from every direction. I would hop fences, sprint through backyards onto a street, run directly into a cop car, turn around, and run the other way.

This went on for a couple of minutes until I realized I was surrounded and there was no way I was going to get out of this. Exhausted, I put my hands on my head, hit my knees and gave up. Despite the fact that I had clearly surrendered, an officer stuck his gun in my face, screaming at me to "get the fuck on the ground!" He pointed the gun at my face for a few until he finally holstered the weapon and stopped yelling. I had half a moment of what I thought was calm until he punched me in the face and cuffed me.

I spent a total of twenty-two days between my second release from prison and heading back to prison for the third time. I thanked the universe that I left that .45 in the glove box.

Chapter Six

Sentence enhancements for being a gang member, a repeat offender, and for committing habitual criminal acts had me staring at ten to fifteen years in prison. I wasn't going to give in to a full decade in prison. I rationalized that I had not committed violent crimes against people. My case was just another run of the mill grand theft auto. I had been through this before and knew that if I held out I could get a better deal. I also knew that trials and appeals are expensive propositions for the state. For small cases like mine, they prefer to cut a plea bargain.

I held out for months awaiting trial while the D.A. built his case. Every so often he would come with a proposal for a plea bargain – eight years, seven years, five, then three and a half.

I wanted two years and was ready to keep holding out for that but my public defender – already aghast and fed up with my defiance –

pushed me to take the deal. I was satisfied with that.

They shipped me to a prison in Jamestown, about two hours east of San Francisco. I was far from friends and family, but I was mostly estranged from them at this point. Having disappointed my family once again, the isolation didn't really matter to me. I was better off removed from any emotional ties that would hold me back. Plus, with two prison terms under my belt, I had credibility with the Southerners.

I was in an entirely different headspace that third term. I went up there with the mentality that I was now a career criminal. It was time to make a name for myself. In the past five years I had lived a total of forty-one days on the street. The street was like a vacation–women, drugs, and bullshit to get into. Prison was like going to work, and that is how I approached it. I was going to focus more on prison politics this time, and put in the work to rise in the ranks. I looked at it like I was climbing the ladder of a Fortune 500 company. I tattooed my entire body with crude gangland tattoos – pictures of demons and skulls, representations of the street and the darkness that I was living in. I even tattooed both sides of my head. On one side I have "San Pedro" and on the other "Any Bitch Can Be Replaced."

I accepted this as a way of life. The bars no longer had the ominous presence about them. They were simply scenery in my environment, like a couch in the living room. The bars would be my future. I accepted that. These thoughts swirled in my head right before intake. I had a flashback to my childhood when I desperately wanted to be someone when I grew up. Here it is. This is my calling and I am going to ride it out until it kills me. I thought that would be fulfilling, it wasn't. But I couldn't face that in the moment, and so I shook it off like the cold.

Once I was settled into my unit, I volunteered myself for any missions the gang needed done. Some of those missions were of high caliber, and some were what I classify as assignments for crash-test dummies – suicide missions given to the least intelligent and disposable members. I had a big problem with that. There was no way I was going to be anybody's crash-test dummy, but I'm a soldier, and doing what I'm told is how to rise in the ranks.

That conflict stewed inside me, and I had a lot of time to think about it during my trip to the hole after my first major riot of this term, which occurred nearly a year and a half into my sentence. This riot was with a Northside gang (the Mexicans from Northern California who were often warring with the Mexicans from Southern California) on the A yard. There had been tension brewing over the past six months between the two gangs.

The hole is prison inside prison. It is exactly what it sounds like. Inmates who violate prison rules are locked up in solitary confinement twenty-four/seven. Other than a guard sliding a tray of food into my cell I had no contact with other human beings. I remembered an old saying I used to hear the dockworkers say – "A fish doesn't know what water is until he is out of it." I did not realize how important human contact was until I was isolated from it. I had only my thoughts to keep me company. It was dangerous company. In a place filled with rapists, thieves, and murderers, the worst thing you can do is leave a man by himself.

By this time, my family started talking to me again and I was having calls with my mom, Toni, and Danielle. They suspended my calls when I was in the hole, and I actually missed them. It was an odd emotion to come back to me, and I didn't really know what to do with it, but I tried to acknowledge and face it the best I could. While isolated, I became much more introspective. Surprisingly, my thoughts weren't as dark as I'd thought they'd be. They were much more cerebral. A whisper inside me began questioning the life I was living, and the life I always had lived. I kept going back and forth between being stoked that I was getting recognition for my part in the riot, and thinking I was being played as a puppet. I wanted to do something that would allow me to prove myself, but I was not about to take the fall for others. In the quiet and stillness of that room, and my mind, I realized I had been struggling with this conflict since my tagging days as a kid.

***

The prison was divided into yards A and B of about 38 dorms housing 40 men to a dorm. Each yard had a mix of Mexicans (Northsiders and Southsiders), Blacks (Crips and Bloods), Whites (Peckerwoods and Skinheads) and others. When I got out of the hole, guys gave me respect for doing my part in the riot. One individual told me to "set the yard off again" if I found myself on the same yard we just rioted on. I felt accomplished in my purpose and thought it to be an honor that they asked me to set the yard off again. But my inner voice spoke to me saying "Why did they ask you?" The thought startled me, as if it had originated from outside of my body. I never once asked myself that critical question – why?

News in prison spreads fast. T, the Southside shotcaller knew I was going back to the A yard before I left the hole, before I knew. I wasn't back in my dorm thirty minutes before I got the note from T. All it said was "set the yard off." I knew exactly what I was supposed to do. As soon as I hit yard A, I was to attack as many of the Northside guys as I could, and set off another riot. I held that note and ran through all the possibilities of what might happen. Maybe they'll put me away for life. Maybe they'll kill me. Regardless of what happened, I knew this was supposed to be my moment. I thought, "If I carry this out, I'll rise in rank, maybe even become a shotcaller. I will be untouchable. But there is no coming back from this." If I carried this out, the gang life would be the only life I would ever know, and gangsters rarely retire.

I should've been excited, but I was torn. Then Jay said very briefly and directly, the most powerful words I could've heard in that moment: "They're playing you for a sheep." Those words shook my reality. I froze and turned to Jay. I couldn't even get a word out in response because what he was saying was true. What I had been asked to do was not a political move given to someone whose destiny was to become a leader. There wasn't even a reason behind calling for a riot. It wouldn't help our cause in any way; it was called just for the hell of it. These were orders given to a crash-test dummy. The guys at the top knew it was a kamikaze mission and gave the orders from the safety of their cell. They weren't the ones who would kill or be killed. There would be no time added to their sentences.

The next day I couldn't eat breakfast. I looked up from a Styrofoam bowl of microwaved oatmeal and saw Jay staring at me. It wasn't the usual stare gangsters give each other before something is about to go down. It was the stare of a friend looking at another friend, wondering what he's going to do when the moment we both know is looming, arrives. "Let's go, single file!" This was the time. I was already too far-gone. Whether it was a kamikaze mission or a step on the ladder to becoming a shotcaller, I didn't know, but orders were orders. I just wished my head would shut up, but once the door to the light of truth is opened, it's impossible to shut it again.

I walked onto the yard with Jay, staring at my feet kicking dirt as I engaged in a mental debate with myself. Jay stopped. I stopped too, confused. Then I saw a skinny Northside kid I recognized from the first prison riot. "This is it," I thought. "One of us is supposed to attack."

Instead, he stuck his hand out. "I apologize for what happened in the yard, man. I hope we can put that behind us and move on." Baffled, I stood looking at him for a second too long. I could see he began to wonder whether I was going to shake his hand, or pull out a shank.

"It's cool," I said.

If I thought I was in a bad headspace before I went onto the yard, I was in an even worse one after I might as well have shook his hand. I had blatantly disobeyed orders. But in the bigger picture, that was my first step on my path to redemption. I spent the next few weeks depressed in my cell. I was totally alone now, as the path tends to be. My head was tearing me apart – telling me one minute I did a good thing, then the next filling me with paranoia that my crew would find out and put a hit on me.

No one from my crew ever found out. By some miracle it slipped through the cracks, but I didn't know that. I spent many sleepless nights with a shank under my pillow, convinced this was the night they would come for me. But they never did, and the only person I was at war with was myself. My enemy had been between my ears for so long, feeding me bad information, convincing me that the life I was living was the path to success and fortune. This time around, it was giving me different information. My brain rerouted its flow of thoughts to a different stream.

I wasn't sure where these thoughts were coming from, but I credited them to the sum of all the minutes, days, and years in my life that I spent incarcerated. When you're in jail, all you have is time to kill. You spend a lot of time with yourself – most of it reading and sitting in introspection. You develop a base of knowledge and education about yourself - if nothing else - that you don't get while you are running on the streets. All the time I had spent in prison – sitting, thinking, and contemplating – built up over the years. The feelings and doubts that were conjured up slowly began to leak from the mental dam I built to contain them. Eventually the dam gave way and I started to see things from an entirely different perspective. Questions and suspicions about my life and memories of my family – specifically my mother – followed the parade of thoughts that marched through my head.

My mother gave me a second chance at life. She took me in, she raised me, she always provided a nurturing, loving home for me to live in. I remembered how she used to pack me lunch with a little note saying she loved me. When I got out of jail, she picked me up and housed me until I broke her heart and went off on another run. And for all of that, I was giving her nothing back. The path I was on was getting narrow. Whatever light left at the end of the tunnel was shrinking quickly. Life in prison or face down on a San Pedro street was going to be my destiny. That was going to be my legacy to my mother. I felt smothered in a thick of remorse.

When I was younger, I accepted the tradeoff that my family would hate me in exchange for my neighborhood and gang loving and respecting me. As the prospect of spending the rest of my life in prison became a likelier probability, the old idea of hood immortality began to look like a mirage. I started to see the stupidity and pointlessness of the gangster life. We spend a tiny fraction of our lives actually out on the street hustling; the majority of our time is spent locked in a cell, alone. We miss birthdays, weddings, deaths, all in the name of our gang and at the end of it all we end up in a box – either concrete or wooden. We never reach the kind of power we think we will achieve. We don't become like the gangsters we see in the movies. We become a two-paragraph story buried in the back of the L.A. Times, or a talking point for some mayor trying to get tough on crime. But most of all we are pawns in a chess game. The narrative of loyalty and brotherhood, of dying for one another and living as warriors, is a great story to tell a young, disenfranchised kid who is looking to fit in somewhere. And then it all came together. Pieces of a puzzle I had been trying to figure out my entire life finally snapped together. Things became clear and true.

Even if I did become like one of the famous gangsters I grew up idolizing, I'd still be a *nobody*. My family would still disown me. My mother would still be heartbroken and disappointed. No matter how rich and famous I became, I would still let my mother down. I would be empty. I never gave life a decent effort, even when I was a kid. I always looked for the shortcuts. I had to try something different – to put some effort into life. At least to show my mother that I gave this thing a real shot. Whether I was successful or not didn't matter. There was also a looming fear that my mother would pass away while I was in prison. I told Toni I was scared I'd be in jail when Mom died. She said to me, "Why don't you just stay out of prison then?"

The thought struck me that I had never done anything to give back to my family – essentially life was all about me. Self-centeredness had consumed me. I had always acted from a fear of what other people thought of me. I used people as tools to achieve what I thought I wanted. My eyes opened up to the lies of what was my reality. Once I was aware of them, I couldn't look the other way.

The last six months of my three-year sentence were to be served in the Los Angeles County jail, which was a final jab in the ribs the district attorney gave me for all the trouble I put him through. County jail is much wilder than prison due to how new and early in the process the inmates are.

Prison inmates are settled in; it has become their home. Guys in jail haven't even been sentenced. They are full of emotions – anger, rage, hate, hopelessness – and are looking for anyone to vent them on. I would have to be hypervigilant to make sure I didn't get caught up in a mess from which there would be no return. I had made the decision I was done with this life, but this final stretch would be the hardest hoop to jump through, before I could get to the other side.

We made the twelve-hour trip by bus from Jamestown state prison to Los Angeles county jail.

My mind was clear the whole time. I had a weight lifted off my shoulders. It was like I finally saw color again, when before all I could see was black and white.

I was booked into building four - as the building's shotcaller was approaching his release date. The Southsiders now needed a leader to run the building – a major position that carried responsibility for a lot of men. I knew he was going to ask me to take his place. I was experienced, I was in the third year of my third term, I had been to penitentiaries all over the state, and I was coming from a state prison. But I respectfully declined. Although I never told him the true reason why, my mind was made up.

Then he told me if I didn't want the position, he was going to give it to Tonto. "Tonto" means dummy in Spanish. Tonto was not all there in the head. He was young and crazy, and well, his nickname was Tonto. He wasn't exactly a genius. This was like going on a road trip and asking the drunkest guy to drive the car. I still had time left on my sentence and I was not to fond of the idea that part of it would be in the hands of a guy named Slow.

I went back to the outgoing shotcaller and told him I would take over. I had to – I wanted to get out of that place alive – and I figured who better to be calling the shots than me. I could be master of my own fate. The building was filled with young, first timers to jail. They didn't understand how the system operated, and were constantly getting into trouble – drawing heat to our unit. They made me nervous.

It was difficult for me to run the building with the mindset I was in. I had a major position of authority but was mentally checked out. I didn't have the inner anger and frustration that it takes to be a committed and ruthless shotcaller. I was just trying to skate through these six months unscathed by either the prison system, or a mutiny from my own crew. But I couldn't escape the reality: I was in charge of a small unit of the largest prison gang in California. There wasn't going to be any skating by. Tough decisions had to be made.

***

I was getting ready to play a pinochle game. We were in a dorm-style barracks – about fifty to seventy guys sleeping in cots in a large open room. It was that mellow time after dinner and before bed where guys would usually play cards or participate in some kind of game for money or commissary. Earlier in the day the guards searched the dorm, looking for drugs and other illegal items. The guards gave me extra shit during these searches because they knew I ran the building. The officers spend so much time in prison that they become as much a part of the environment as the inmates. They pick up information, hear the gossip and see the messages being passed. They have developed the same kind of intuition the prisoners have. They can feel when something is about to go down, just like we can. The prisoners and guards depend on a collective mistrust of one another. It motivates both groups to be better at what they do. Part of that mistrust was giving extra shit to the shotcallers. I understood and respected that; both of our jobs called for it. During this search, the guards pulled aside and harassed one of the younger inmates in my unit. He mouthed off to them, and they beat his ass.

As I was sitting on my bunk, the young inmate bursts into the dorm with a full head of steam, a busted lip, and a black eye. He started tripping out, screaming and cursing about the cops roughing him up during the search. He stomped around the dorm, hitting people's possessions off the shelves, and throwing chairs against the wall. His energy was volatile and unpredictable. The first thing that popped into my head was the old man's voice from my very first time in jail – "and you don't fuck with the guards!"

These kids had no concept of how the system worked. All they wanted to do was get into prison and fuck things up. They had a mentality of violence, aggression, and destruction that was familiar, but distant from my current mindset. I could relate to this kid. I knew where his head was at, but I wasn't in touch with that anymore. I couldn't channel it or feel it with any sort of passion.

That was a scary place to be in. I was out of my element in my own habitat. What had always been natural was now totally foreign to me. I was floating in a purgatory, and in that moment I had no allegiance to anyone but myself. I just knew I had to keep swimming towards the light – the good. Like a soldier in a foxhole daydreaming of home, the rush of heat that comes in the presence of intense aggression snapped me out of my trance. Like an actor being put in the spotlight, I had to perform.

"Ay homie, all right, sit down. So, what do you want to do about it?" I said.

One thing gangbangers know – regardless of how green they are – is that they are to respond to a shotcaller's direction. The split-second thought he gave my question was a long enough pause to get him to calm down.

"Sit down," I said.

He sat on the cot across from me, then I heard the crash of a steel door slamming against a concrete wall. Standing in the doorway was the guard that had conducted the search.

"Rodriguez! Where ya at?!" the guard screamed into the unit from the doorway. He didn't dare walk in; the gang dominated the unit.

"If you don't come out, I'm gonna fucking drag you out!"

People stood up one by one from bunks, tables, and chairs. The guys watching TV turned around and stood. The guys playing cards put down their cards and looked at the guard. The room became tense. Anger and hostility was fermenting into something dangerous. The guard left, soon returning with two more guards, who came in with authority.

Everybody in the unit was on their feet. The young inmate shouted at the three guards, "This is our house! We fuckin' live here!" Like revolutionaries rising against an occupying force, the inmates shouted in agreement. They began ripping shirts to put over their face to guard themselves from the tear gas that would come. Some filled socks with bars of soap, others pulled out makeshift weapons they had stashed away. All I could think about was how I wish I were anywhere but here.

More guards arrived, lining up outside the dorm in full riot gear with tear gas guns and rubber pellet rifles. The guys in my unit were pumped, ready for war. I just wanted to go home. I knew how this situation would go down. The dorm room would turn into a warzone. A lot of people were going to get hurt, and a couple may be killed, including me.

The guards know who the shotcallers of every unit are and that we have to give the green light on any action taken by the gang. A revolt of about seventy men would have to be crushed with an overkill of force for no other reason than to send a message to other inmates that this wouldn't be tolerated. The hammer would fall hardest on the shotcaller who gave his blessing to such an outrageous and defiant act. I'd heard of past riots that were smaller, but where the cops still beat the shotcaller to death. A letter to the inmate's family would say how their son was killed in self-defense during a riot. This would probably be my fate, right as I was about to be released with the serious conviction to change my life. Then a short, stocky lieutenant, who looked like a Marine drill instructor, entered. He barged through the line of cops, holding a cup of coffee, shouting as he walked up and down the aisles of cots.

"You motherfuckers wanna do this? If I spill a single drop of this coffee you're all FUCKED!"

I prayed that no one would hit him, thus setting off a bomb that would've killed or maimed most of us. A second guard who trailed the lieutenant said, "All right, let us speak to your representative, let's sort this out." It was a voice of reason, in a room wound so tight, it nearly strangled everyone in it.

Every gang unit has its own negotiator. In our case, it was a well-spoken, intelligent kid named

Danny. Under other circumstances, he would have made a good lawyer or politician. The negotiator deals with the guards' chosen spokesperson. They advocate on behalf of their groups to keep the peace and broker deals in the mutual interest of everyone that lives and works behind those concrete walls.

I sent Danny to talk with the guards. They spoke for a couple of minutes, as I stayed off to the side, pacing back and forth with all the possibilities of what could happen running through my head. When Danny came back into the dorm, I pulled him aside before anyone could ask him questions.

We sat down on adjacent bunks, away from everyone else.

"How did it go down?" I said.

"I told them the officers were out of hand. They assaulted one of ours with no reasonable cause. It wasn't self-defense, they weren't detaining him. The lieutenant was pissed. He agreed with, and understood, our position. He said he would investigate on his own. He knows we don't snitch and didn't even bother to ask for names."

"Okay," I said, looking to my second in command. "Good enough? Or you wanna go to war?"

He assured me that we had made our stand. An all-out riot against the guards was unnecessary, and at this point would just be outright foolish. We had secured a rare victory over the authorities through diplomatic means.

We agreed, and to my relief the young kid who was the cause of the situation chimed in.

"We made a big enough statement," he said.

I made it through the most difficult test of fire I had faced, and I came out the other side unscathed. I was an emotional wreck from the ordeal, but I would shake that off in time. I was alive. Regardless of how long my odds were, I was still in the game.

Chapter Seven

A warm wind smacked me in the face through the open window of Mike's girl's Honda. Mike, who had lived two cells down from me, was a biker in his thirties who was locked up for a string of robberies in the South Bay. We weren't close, but we were acquaintances. Mike and I were both released from the county jail at the same time, and he offered me a ride home. They lived two hours in the opposite direction from me, but she didn't have a say in the matter.

The scent of jasmine and salt in the air lulled me into a light sleep, summoned by misty memories of pleasant childhood summers, until a car racing down the 10 freeway startled me back to reality. Wet pavement hissed under the tires. Palm trees, backlit by the moon, flew by my field of vision, their twisted trunks reaching for the sky. The sights, smells, and sounds of the free world, which I hadn't experienced in three years, overloaded my senses. I was in a state of shell shock, gratitude, and fear that comes with returning after exile from the world.

"You need to use the phone?" Mike asked.

"Yeah, I need to call my mom."

My call woke her up but she didn't sound bothered. "Hi Mom, I just got out. I'm on my way home."

"Okay, I'll leave the door open," she replied.

Mike dropped me off and we said our goodbyes. He told me to hit him up when I got back in the game, and I told him I would. Inside, I hoped I would never see his face again.

Mom was sitting at the table in her pajamas, having a cup of coffee with my dad when I walked in. After hugging each other, we sat down and talked. Coming home this time around was much different. It was the middle of the night, quiet and still. In the past I had gotten out during the day and by the time I made it back to the neighborhood there was usually a block party going on. Someone would call me over for drinks, and people were mid stride in their hustles. I would jump back in the mix immediately. My mom used to have a big celebration with the family, taking me out to my favorite place to eat. It was a big deal when I came back from jail, and I felt like I had to make up for lost time.

Those days were over. We had done that dance too many times before, and I was now twenty-three. Mine had been a lifetime of in and out of jail, hellos and goodbyes, tears of leaving and celebrations of returning. My parents were older now too, and the energy in the kitchen was a tired one. I could see they were much less emotionally invested in my homecoming than in the past. It was very nonchalant – like "Chris is home from prison again, let's give him a warm meal, make up the bed, and hope the best." In that kitchen emptiness washed over me. I couldn't do this anymore. I never wanted to come home from prison again.

I knew for that to be even remotely possible, I had to change everything about myself. It would be like learning how to walk again. In the past I always had the mindset that I could smoke a little weed and have a beer here and there. I figured I could hustle a little bit on the side, cause hey, I gotta do what I gotta do to get by. I just had to be careful and lay low for a while. Usually strung out and homeless by the end of the week and in jail before the month was the over, I had the evidence that it was not going to work.

This time around, I became a recluse and my carefulness bordered on paranoia. I didn't leave my house for the first few weeks, and didn't answer the phone for a much longer time than that. I told my mother to tell people who called for me, "he doesn't live here anymore, and I don't know where he is."

After about a month I reemerged, but was still cautious about who I would see and where I would go. I only saw family – Freddy, my nephew David, my sister Toni, and my other cousins. However, I was thrown out into the world by the desperate need for a job, an essential part of changing my life. I wasn't qualified for much but I tried my best. I went to a local shopping center and applied at every single store. I was still very institutionalized and I probably came off a bit scary. I wasn't very good in real world social settings yet, and I struggled to make eye contact with people.

I didn't get any callbacks from the fifty-odd applications. I was preparing myself for the frustration of failure and waiting for the spark that would burn the whole thing to the ground again, but my mother was relentless in her tough-love encouragement. She wouldn't accept no for an answer. It didn't matter to her if I got fifty rejections – send out fifty more. She never tolerated my self-pity and eventually I didn't either.

Opportunities slowly opened for me. I enrolled in occupational school for HVAC (heating and air conditioning) training and took odd jobs around town to make money – digging backyard trenches, cleaning houses, printing T-shirts. If it was not illegal I would take the job. Things were going well. I was sober. I wasn't staying out late running in the streets. But I still carried a cumbersome guilt. I felt like I was playing catch up, and I had a lot of remorse over the choices I made. Ghosts of my not too distant past swirled around in my head, asking me to reconsider if what I was doing with my life was worth the trouble, or if I was already too far gone. But if you asked my family how I was doing, they would say, "Chris is doing great, we're so proud of him."

**

In 2010, I was two years out of prison and I finally caught a break. Our cousins lived across the street in a beautiful 1920s-style plantation home that they turned into a venue for weddings and other events. As a kid, I used to run around their backyard, a huge garden with rows of flowers and white-laced fencing around the perimeter. They called it the Sepulveda Home.

Business was picking up for them and they asked me to help out. It was a conditional, temporary position at first. I think they wanted to see if I was responsible enough to hold down a job and not get in trouble. I washed dishes, filled water dispensers, and did any menial job that no one else wanted to do. I was a good worker and didn't complain. I was motivated the fear that told me everything was going to come crashing down if I screwed this up. Eventually they hired me full time, and from there I got plugged in with catering companies who would come to do events. I started working events for those companies as well.

Working for both the Sepulveda Home, and caterers, I was making good money. My hours increased and so did my responsibilities. I became a staple in both businesses. Every paycheck I received, I was amazed that it had my name on it. More so, I couldn't believe these people trusted me to run my own events and manage their teams. I wanted to ask them, "do you have any idea who I am, or where I've come from?" I followed orders and ran the catering crews like little gangs. We were efficient. I never had so much money saved up in my life. I wasn't drinking, doing drugs or going out to party. All I did was work and save money.

Eventually I went to bartending school so I could bartend at events. I was working all sorts of insane hours and began to burn out, but since I never had an honest job in my life, I chalked it up to life experience. I figured this was what earning money was like.

I grew to dislike the job and hours I was working, but the one thing that kept me motivated was seeing my mother proud of me. I could see it in her eyes, and in the half smile she wore. I had finally fulfilled some essence of the promise to her that I would do something with my life. I had an answer to that question I had always asked myself: "What have you given your mother to be proud of?" The promise and that answer were all that mattered to me. It gave me the strength to push through any stress. I had tunnel vision. Even though I didn't really like the job, I pushed for raises and more responsibilities. Every time I got them, I got to see her face light up when I told her.

Another woman came into my life around this time. I had been dating a woman named Tasha for the better part of a year and things had become serious. I met Tasha in Laughlin, Nevada. Several of my cousins and other friends from the neighborhood would go there to party. We would ride Jet Skis and hang out on the river in the spring and summer. It was a nice get-away from the city. On one of these trips, my buddy brought his wife, who brought her friend, Tasha. The first time I saw her, I was packing a cooler at the hotel, ready to go out on the lake for the day. She walked up with my friend's wife, and I locked eyes with her as I looked up from dumping a package of Coca-Colas into the cooler. She was wearing a white tank top and jean shorts. I could see a pink bikini tied in a knot underneath her shirt. She was a little shorter than me, and her brunette hair bounced with the rhythm of her stride as she walked. Faint streaks of blonde reflected sunlight. She glowed. Her energy was potent and it emanated from the crown of her head.

As I looked up from the cooler, I saw my own reflection in her rose gold, tinted sunglasses.

I tried to say something, but nothing came out.

"Hey! I'm Tasha," she said.

"Chris. Nice to meet you," I replied.

It took every ounce of my energy and willpower to force those words through my dry, chapped lips. I had spent many years of my life surrounded by only men.

The girls got their things, and we finished packing the truck, and left for the lake. I volunteered to drive – nearly insisted on it – because I needed to gather my thoughts and calm myself down. Tasha had me spinning. By the time we arrived at the lake, I was in much better shape. The drive had calmed my nerves. We spent the day on the lake, riding Jet Skis, eating lunch, and enjoying one another's company. For me, there was no one else there but Tasha. We talked the entire time, exchanging our life experiences. I even felt comfortable enough to tell her about my past. I told her where I had been in my life, and explained the process of change I was going through. She never judged me. She told me she was in school and wanted to be a teacher. I never even graduated high school.

We are very different people, opposites one might say, if you were to look at us on paper. But as different as we are, we are equally similar. Love is a series of paradoxes like that. We are both open and honest, and have no problem expressing how we truly feel. We have similar tastes in music, hard rock and metal, and we both were trying to be better people, despite our different starting points. We hit it off right away and spent the rest of the trip at the lake together. When we got back to San Pedro, I moved into her place a couple months later.

Every time I left the house, my pops would ask me where I was going. He was always worried about me, asking who I was going to be with, what I was going to be doing. After a few weeks he asked, somewhat surprised, "This the same girl you've been seeing?" I think he was shocked that I had a steady girlfriend.

Mom met Tasha as we were about to go on a camping trip. She came by the house to pick me up. My mother answered the door. They didn't speak for long but my mom saw the same light in her eyes that I did, her positive energy that radiates from within. After that vacation Tasha and I did everything together. She even began coming to our Wednesday night dinners, when my mother would cook for our whole family. That was a big deal.

My mother loved her. "I've seen the girls you use to bring around here. She's a sweetheart, Chris." She was happy for Tasha and me, and Tasha became a source of comfort for my mother. Mom knew that I was on the right track with a girl like her, and with the other pieces of my life coming together, things were trending in the right direction.

The seeds of change I had planted within myself – that I took a gamble on – in the cold, infertile ground of the prison yard, started to sprout. Four years out of prison, I was a different person. Not only did I change my outside appearances by getting a job, paying bills on time, and learning other basic life skills, but I changed what was inside of me as well.

I began to look outward, toward others. I saw life in new hues. It was like walking out of prison all over again and seeing the world in color after seeing only grey and white prison walls. I cared about my family and my mother. I showed up for my job and was a good employee. I became loving, caring, and compassionate towards other people. A range of emotions that I had suppressed my entire life began to blossom. In 2012 my life was the best it had ever been. For the first time in my life I had a sense of stability.

***

The first hint that something wasn't right was when my mother told us that she wasn't feeling well. She would look at us with an unsettled expression and rub the back of her head. Then she would ask one of us to rub the back of her head. It felt like a marble.

"I don't know, you should get it checked, Ma," I'd tell her.

Before I was born, my mother had won a bout against breast cancer. She went through all the treatments, had a double mastectomy, and the cancer went into remission. Over twenty years later she was diagnosed with lung cancer. I was at my mom's house after work when she came home from the doctors and told us the diagnosis. The wind was sucked out of me. My mother is tough. She told me in a matter of fact way.

"We are going to start treatment and talk to the doctors," she said, sitting across from me at the kitchen table.

I felt like a helpless little kid. I wanted to cry but I couldn't let out any tears. I was lost and scared, and then ashamed that I was scared. I wanted to do something, but I couldn't do anything; I tried to think of what I could do to make this not be real.

The rest of that winter and the following spring were miserable. I was coming apart from the stress. I was taking care of my mother and trying to be present with her. I took her to every doctor and treatment appointment. I kept track of her medications and made sure she took them properly. I was working and had more responsibilities and events to do than ever before.

The stress in my family was boiling over those few months. Mom was the center of the family. She was the glue that held everyone together, and the engine that kept us pushing forward. The whole family dynamic was thrown into chaos. Toni, Freddy, the cousins, and all her grandchildren were feeling the pressure as much as I was. It was hard on everybody. Towards the end my mom's condition deteriorated rapidly. She was receiving chemotherapy and taking an assortment of medications. We all pitched in to take her to appointments every week, but the treatments progressively stopped working. Her breathing became softer and shallower. I had to help her walk in and out of doctors' offices. She was barely hanging on.

June 19th, 2012 was my twenty-sixth birthday. My mother was sleeping in my bedroom at the time because she could no longer walk up the stairs to her own. The June gloom overcast of Los Angeles was thick that day and it was slightly chilly. We had family over for a barbecue to celebrate my birthday, as well as enjoy time with Mom. By then, we knew that our time with her was limited. I was sitting on the back patio having a conversation with my cousins and nephews when my brother walked out.

He said to us in a muffled voice, clearly trying to hold back tears, "Okay guys, I think it is about that time."

I started to crumble, but I gathered myself and followed my family into Mom's bedroom.

She was lying on the bed, working hard to breathe. Surrounding her, we took turns holding her hand, saying goodbye. I struggled to find something to say. I pulled at words, ones like those she had spoken to me so calmly months before.

"I'm scared, Mom, I love you. I love you."

"I don't know what you're afraid of. Don't be scared. I'm not scared. I'm ready. I've done everything I need to do," she replied.

Now at her bedside, I thanked her for everything she had done for me. There was little else to say. I kept thinking of how strong she had been throughout her life, especially the last few months. I was trying to draw from that strength because I was collapsing inside. It was difficult to slow down my thoughts and emotions; so much was going through my head.

When I got out of prison, I felt like I was walking into the woods in the middle of the night. It was a long path through those woods. The dark played tricks on me. I was scared and didn't know if I would be able to make it through, but I had the most important tool for this journey - a flashlight. That light gave me serenity and peace of mind. It led the way, guiding me to place one foot in front of the other, otherwise the dark would have swallowed me. Whenever the woods became too frightening, or my head began telling me stories of what awaits behind the trees, I'd remember the flashlight and feel safe again.

As I watched my mother take her last breaths, I saw her eyes grow dim. I watched the light of her soul – my flashlight – go out. And I knew I would have to keep moving forward, through the woods, without a light. But before I moved forward I had to curl up and lie down for a while. Now was a time for mourning, there would be a time to push on later.

At the wake I couldn't stop looking at her in the casket. It was like I was stuck in a trance. I just couldn't believe it was her lying there. My sister Toni was having a tough time saying goodbye, and everyone was distraught as they lined up to pay their respects. This woman meant so much to a lot of people.

"I can't believe that's her," I said to Freddy.

He replied, "That's not her. She's with God now." I found some relief in that.

My nephew David gave the eulogy at her funeral and asked each of us to write something.

I wrote, "Even though she didn't give birth to me, she gave me life. She saved me as a child coming out of the foster care system, and as an adult she saved me from myself."

Chapter Eight

Even in the darkest reaches of my depression, the thought to turn back to the streets or drugs and alcohol never entered my mind. Although I didn't realize it in that pain-filled time following my mother's death, I had turned a corner. The seeds of change had grown roots deep enough to hold strong while I sat through the ache that ripped through my heart over the next six to eight months. I sat in the darkness of my mom's passing for a while, not knowing where to go. I was lost, and waves of apathy became part of the depression engulfing me. I felt like everything was gone, and there was not much worth caring about anymore.

At first I didn't take any events at work. After a couple weeks I began to work again, but not in any consistent manner. I wasn't thriving anymore. I was no longer hungry. Life went from full color to gray scale.

Physically, I was deteriorating. I had no appetite and couldn't sleep. Memories of my mother – regrets, joys, celebrations – they rolled like a film reel through my brain, keeping me up all night. I slept through the day. The combination of lack of food and sleep took a toll on me. I began to lose my mind. I wasn't all there. My depression grew worse and I lost a lot of weight. My family and Tasha were worried for my physical and mental health.

Some days Tasha would do her best to get me out of bed in the morning. "Come on, babe. Just give it a try today," she'd say. I would roll over and wait for her to leave for work. I'd spend the rest of the day lying in bed with the shades drawn in, not leaving until night fell. Tasha would come home from work and find me in a similar position as when she left nine hours ago. I knew it was breaking her heart, but I could not pull myself out. Then worry crept in about whether or not I would take my own life.

My mother was already looking out for me from above. She sent me a life preserver in a place I least expected it. I was pumping gas at the 76 on the corner of Third Street in San Pedro, watching the winter rain fall when a familiar face walked out of the convenience store. It was Ray, my mom's next door neighbor. We exchanged hellos and he gave me his condolences. We exchanged laughs over old memories, and he told me how he always remembered my mom volunteering at the school for Hamburger Tuesdays.

Then he said, "I've been hitting the gym a lot, man. I go to MetroFlex down in Long Beach. It's hardcore in there, you would dig it. You should check it out." That simple and seemingly insignificant phrase would change my life. I told him I would give him a call, and we went our separate ways. I was not into fitness at the time, and never had been. For some reason, Ray's words stuck in my mind, swirling around for several days. The idea didn't really excite me, but the fact he called it a "hardcore facility" caught my ear.

I remembered the prison workouts the gang members would do together. Every time I was feeling stressed and exercised, I felt better afterward. I sold myself on the idea to go check out MetroFlex. I needed something to give me relief, otherwise I was on the path to imploding and self destructing. I wanted to sleep at night. I wanted to not think about killing myself during the day. Even the slightest relief would be a massive success. I would get that relief and more, beyond anything I imagined.

I showed up at MetroFlex one night after work around six o'clock. It was a huge old warehouse, and exercise equipment stretched as far as I could see. At the front of the gym was a sprawling section of cardio equipment. Behind it, extending all the way to the back of the gym, were free weights, bench presses, and squat racks. Flags of the different branches of the military hung from the ceiling, and massive murals of super-hero-like men busting through the cement filled the walls. I had never seen a gym like this. The people working out were hyper focused. They didn't see or hear anyone. Nothing mattered except the rep they were doing. The men were huge, and the women beautiful. Everyone was wearing tight neon gym clothes that looked straight out of the Nike catalog.

I walked into this scene with my baggy black AND1 basketball shorts, a white wife beater, and some old Air Forces. I felt so uncomfortable I thought my body was going to leap out of my skin. It was just as intimidating as the first time I walked onto a prison yard. I sheepishly tried to navigate my way through the sprawling gym floor, sidestepping and shimmying past people bench pressing and deadlifting. It took me five minutes to get to the free weight rack that lay across the back wall. It felt like it took five days. I was dizzy. I leaned on the weight rack to gather my nerves. Right before I bent over to pick up a twenty-pound dumbbell, the thought occurred to me – no one cared. No one stopped to stare at me or made me feel unwelcome. There was no hostility whatsoever. Everyone was doing their own thing. I took a deep breath, wore a half smile – which I had not felt in a while – and began.

I had no idea what I was doing. My workouts were a combination of some crude exercises I learned in prison, mimics of workouts I saw others doing, and staple exercises like bench press and curls from Phys. Ed. class. But I fell in love with it that first night. The entire scene amazed me: bodybuilders who looked sculpted out of marble, power lifters raising Atlas loads of weight. Every time I turned my head, I saw something I had never seen before. It blew my mind. I felt that same joy and freedom as when I was released from prison – only this time the prison was my head.

I became addicted to the gym. I went every day for the first two weeks until a guy told me I should rest a couple of days to allow my body to heal. I took it down to five days a week and got into a rhythm. My health and well-being improved those first few weeks. I finally slept at night. The suicidal ideations ceased, and I was in an overall better mood. My sister and Tasha weren't so worried about me anymore. It made their lives easier seeing that I found some relief.

I would wake up when Tasha did and leave for the gym as she left for work. She would come home, and I would be running errands and doing odd jobs around the house. We were laughing together and joking around for the first time in months. The more I worked out, the happier I was, and the happier she was watching me pull myself out of my darkness.

As I kept showing up to Metroflex, I made friends. I got very close to the owner, Eddie, who took the time to show me new workouts. When he saw me coming regularly, he knew I was dedicated, but my technique was as graceful as a car crash. He gave me some tips, mostly so I wouldn't hurt myself.

I came into the gym on an unusually hot Saturday afternoon in the beginning of 2013. The back of the gym had an extra wide garage door, used at some point for trucks to come in and out of the warehouse. The door was wide open. Sunlight and warm air rushed in, lighting up the gym floor. I was used to seeing it under fluorescent lights, which made it look like a dungeon. The illumination provided the space with a sacred feeling.

The gym was nearly empty, and I was half working out and half watching what a group of guys were doing in the doorframe. As I grabbed a dumbbell off the rack, I saw a man doing a muscle up on the bar. He raised himself up to a pull up, floated above the bar, and then dropped back down in place. "What the hell was that?" I thought. He was six inches taller than me and weighed at least thirty pounds more but he had floated in the air.

He did more muscle ups. Every time, he floated, fully suspended in the air. It was graceful, a far cry from the clunky, mechanical exercises I was doing. A guy named Ace ran up to the bar and swiftly jumped into a hanging position. He did the same muscle up, but he did a 360-degree rotation in the air. I watched other guys take turns on the bar, each of them doing moves more impressive than the last.

I had no idea what I was looking at, but I loved it. I felt like a caveman trying to start a fire, when someone suddenly flicked a BIC lighter in front of my face. Ace saw me staring and asked if I wanted to try.

"You ever do one?" he said.

I laughed out of nervousness and said, "I don't even know what a muscle up is."

"Watch."

He jumped on the bar, pulled himself up, floated in the air – to me it looked like he had hit the pause button on gravity – and he came back into a hanging position.

"Give it a shot," he said.

My ego, which had emerged from my state of self-pity into a new sense of confidence since I had started working out, spoke to me, "You did mad pull-ups in prison. This is nothin'." I jumped and grabbed onto the bar in a hanging position, my legs slightly swaying. I completed the pull up, and thought I had it just as my eyes came level with the bar, but that is where the motion stopped. I couldn't lift myself from the pull up into a muscle up. Ace gave me a few tips on technique, and I tried again, but I still could not get over the bar.

I was humbled. It was harder than it looked. Ace and the group took off. They told me they trained here all the time, and if I was interested, I could train with them. I was grateful they reached out. I'm naturally very shy, and never would've approached them on my own. This was my first introduction to the sport of calisthenics – using your own body weight to workout. Calisthenics comes from the Greek word Kalos Sthenos, which means beautiful strength. What I saw that day was indeed beautiful.

Over the next week I kept coming back in hopes of seeing them there. I would run into them during late night workouts after most of the rush hour crowd dissipated. They let me work out with them and showed me some techniques on the bars. I was happy just to be working out with them, and I appreciated their kindness and goodwill in taking the time to teach me. I am not sure what they saw in me, but I suspect it was more than I saw in myself at that time.

The following Saturday I crossed paths with them again, but I was coming in as they were leaving. Ace flagged me down.

"Hey bro, you're into this calisthenics thing, aren't you?" he said.

"Yeah, man. I think it's pretty cool."

"Awesome. If you want, come meet us at the beach in Venice tomorrow at two. They have a whole bar set up and a big group of us meets there every Sunday."

"For sure. I'll be there," I said.

An adrenaline shot of excitement coursed through my body from head to toe. For a long time, I never had anything to look forward too. I did not have the slightest idea of what I was going to, but I was ecstatic.

The next day I picked up my friend Sam and we drove to Venice. As I drove, the desire of being accepted by this group became prominent in my head. They were amazing athletes with an aura of positivity. I wanted to be a part of it. I wanted to impress them, so Sam and I left at around eleven. I stopped on the way to get a cooler and cases of water. We got to Venice around noon.

As Sam and I dragged the water and cooler to the beach, we came upon an urban gym that unfolded in front of us. Bars, rings, and Muscle Beach were our playground. And no one was there.

"Okay," I thought. "We are just a little early."

1 p.m. – Still no one there.

2 p.m. - Sam was looking like he was over this, and I was getting sunburnt.

3 p.m. – "Maybe they aren't going to show."

"Fuck."

3:30 p.m. Ace was finally coming over the hill. "Yes! Finally," I exclaimed to Sam, but he still looked over the whole deal.

Ace brought a crew with him. Another twenty people trickled in over the next hour. He introduced me to everyone and as we started working out, I felt like I was a part of the scene. People were laughing and smiling, horsing around as we exercised. The beach popped with life. Tourists stopped and took pictures of us. I was intoxicated by it.

We stayed until dusk. I was burnt bright red and banged up from falling down. Sam looked like he wanted to kill me, but I just wanted more. I compared the feeling to when I was accepted into my gang, and the present one shattered that. The gang world felt like a lifetime ago. This was pure, positive, a feeling of euphoria, brotherhood, and love that I had never felt in a social group. I had finally found my tribe, my thing – my IT. And in all of that – under the hot sun that I paid tribute to with my sweat, in the smiles and laughs of my newfound people, on bars of steel and in the sand that I fell into and picked myself up out of – I found myself.

Chapter Nine

I was finally happy again. I found the feeling of pure excitement and joy of learning something new. It brought me back to being a kid and experiencing things for the first time – sports, girls, parties. I had always corrupted those pure experiences, taken more than my fair share, never been satisfied with what I was given. But I cherished this. I wasn't going to let it slip away.

I trained with the crew at the beach every weekend. Riccardo, Justin, and Ace were my main guys. Although I felt part of the group, as we grew closer, I worried that they would find out about my past. I stressed over what they would think about me if they found out the truth. So I took precautions to hide my past. I grew my hair to cover the tattoos on my head. A fully tattooed person looks rough enough, head tattoos are another other level of abrasiveness. I've been balding since high school, and have always shaved my head, so I began to look like a gangster George Costanza. I was also nervous to work out with my shirt off. I have gang tattoos and anyone familiar with tattoos can tell that my ink was done in prison. I told them bits and pieces of my story, but I spoke generally and vaguely. I eventually dropped the façade, and they became the first guys I let in to see the real me. They accepted me for who I was and who I had been.

They used to joke with me and say, "We didn't know if we should talk to you at first. You're intense looking, and when you work out you look straight up angry. You made a few of us nervous."

Throughout my life, I had longed to fit in and be accepted. I searched for that in gangs and crime, and it ruined me. I was still searching. The longing to be accepted had not changed. But for the first time, I sought acceptance from a positive group of people.

I still worked my day job at the catering company, but fitness consumed me. It was all I thought about, and all I wanted to do. Even at work I worked out. I'd set up a couple chairs and do dips. I would do pulls-ups in doorframes and practice my handstands. My coworkers got a kick out of it. They laughed at first, but told me I was getting better and stronger.

This was typical me. I found something I loved and overdosed on it. I had this extreme, over-do it mindset with gangs, drugs – pretty much everything

I have ever committed to. I always tried to hold myself back, moderate to some degree, but I never could. My brain is just hardwired that way.

I was a shell of a human being when I walked into that MetroFlex in Long Beach. Even though I wasn't actively seeking the street life after my mom died, I was completely apathetic – I just didn't care. With that kind of mindset I was bound to go back to the darkness I had left behind. It was just a matter of crossing paths with the wrong person who asked the right question – "where you been?" "Wanna go grab a drink?" But instead I crossed paths with calisthenics. It saved my life. It breathed life back into my lungs.

I'm always the last one to give myself credit. I had been out of jail for a number of years and managed to keep myself off the streets. I found an honest job I could make into a career. I made my mother and my family proud, and I showed up for them when my mother was sick and passed away. The evidence of my change was all around me, but I was the last one to see it. I finally saw it when I took a step back, and noticed how I was attracting more positive things into my life. Positive activities like fitness and positive people like my new crew were evidence that change was not something I had to strive for, but instead was part of who I was. I made the connection that all these good things would not stick around if I were still that empty, broken guy who walked into the Jamestown correctional facility five years before.

***

What we do is calisthenics by nature because it is all bodyweight movement, but it is specifically influenced by gymnastics. We don't operate competitively in the same way as gymnastics, so we don't use that term. Routines are judged not only on perfection of movement, but also by the individual's expression and style of those movements. Many of the moves and movements we do come from gymnastics. We use the same mediums of high bars, parallel bars, floor, and compete in similar categories, but we bring a creative, street influenced style to it.

I was working out and traveling wherever Ace and the guys went. We trained on the beach in Venice, in Orange County, all over southern California. I always wanted more. The guys would finish a workout and say their goodbyes, and I wanted to know when the next workout was. I was in a groove, feeling comfortable both on the bars and among the people in the scene.

During one of our Sunday morning meetups on Venice Beach, I met Kenneth Gallarzo, – vice president of the World Calisthenics Organization (WCO). Kenneth built the WCO from nothing more than an idea and turned it into the premier organization for calisthenics. They hold fitness expos all over the world and put on most of the major contests, including the pinnacle of calisthenics competition – the Battle of the Bars.

Kenneth was on a higher plane than the average gym goer. His routine on the bars was advanced, and he did movements and exercises with such technique and form that I suspected he was a professional athlete of some type. But what really interested me about Kenneth had nothing to do with fitness. It was his energy. People listened to him and hung on his words. There was the general aura of "that's the guy." Prison taught me to sit back and observe people. I know within seconds who plays what role in a group. I can tell who the big guy on the yard is, and he was it. He has the same magnetic appeal that draws people in which all the great leaders possess.

I listened to him speak and give tips to others on the beach. He was well educated and well spoken. He knew what he was talking about. A lot of people run their mouths and try to be the biggest guy on the yard, but that was not Ken. He just spoke truth and knowledge. It was the product of being a student of fitness. I developed a deep level of respect for him before we even met.

When I introduced myself to him, we hit it off right away. Being as obsessed about the sport as I was, I wanted to learn everything I could. We talked all afternoon. I fired question after question at him about every aspect of the fitness game: nutrition, workouts, physiology. Kenneth had an answer for everything. He told me his story of being a personal trainer, then seeing YouTube videos of guys exercising on bars and being blown away by it. I recognized from that first day that I had to stick close to this guy.

He had proverbs that I loved like, "It's not always about training harder. It's about training smarter." I didn't know how to train smarter. I have one speed – one hundred miles an hour, I'm intense and all I knew was training harder. I wanted to take my training to the next level. But I had to learn more about the sport and my body to do that. Kenneth taught me that knowledge was the other half of this puzzle. Pure physicality can only take you so far. Ken was the guy who could take me to the next phase of my development. He taught a class twice per week at a gym in Hawthorne, and I went to every class.

I had not been to a class in years, I don't even have a high school diploma, but I was hungry for this knowledge. I listened to everything Ken said. He taught about recovery, foam rolling, the proper number of sets and reps. He preached the importance of reading books about the anatomy and physiology of the human body. I began to understand the science of fitness. When I incorporated what I learned into my routine, I saw greater results, transforming my body and my mind.

"This is actually working," I thought. "Not only am I happy, but I am getting good at this.'

The group I was so worried about not accepting me was now saying things like, "Damn Chris, how did you do that move?"

"Damn Chris, I can't even do that."

"Damn Chris, you're progressing."

This fitness thing was taking off. I was at the top of a rollercoaster ride, looking at the waiting drop. Fitness became all that I wanted to do with my life.

Battle of the Bars 2 was coming to San Jose and everyone in the gym, on the beach, and everywhere else we trained, was excited. It seemed like everyone I knew was going to the Fit Expo, and many would be competing, but I couldn't get off work from the catering job. I was really bugged and let down by that, but I continued to train hard and go to class. I was gaining strength and agility, and was one of the best guys at the beach on Sundays.

I would train with Kenneth several times a week. During one session he asked, "Battle of the Bars 3 is coming up – you gonna compete?" I was caught off guard by the question. It took me a minute for my brain to compute what he was saying – that I was good enough for a competition. Kenneth was like that – so direct that sometimes it would knock you off balance.

"I just started. I don't know," I said.

He replied, "We need athletes. You're gonna do good." He left it at that.

Battle of the Bars 3 was being held at the Los Angeles Convention Center in downtown Los Angeles. The L.A. Fit Expo is huge, pulling in 50,000 people over a weekend. The Battle of the Bars was a twofold competition, consisting of One on One battles, in which two guys would compete head to head with the best routine winning and a sixteen-man tournament.

In the weeks preceding the Fit Expo, Ken talked me into competing in the tournament. I was nervous the week leading up to the competition. It was hard for me to sleep some nights. International competitors were flying in from all over the world. But when I voiced my doubts to Ken, he wouldn't hear any of it.

"You HAVE to do it. Not only do I think you're ready – you're gonna win it!" he would say.

"I don't think I'm ready" was not a sufficient answer for him. He believed in me, and my crew echoed that as well. They were my motivation. I still doubted myself, but they believed in me.

Finally, I said "Fuck it, I'm down. Let's do it."

Although I was fearful, I was excited. Everyone in my family is an athlete. The girls play softball, soccer, and basketball; the guys play football and baseball. I grew up hearing stories about Freddy and Uncle Jimmy's gridiron classics. When one of my cousins had a game, the entire family would show up to support them. I never had that experience, and it was always something I felt I had missed out on, something that kept me separate and different in my family. One of the few times someone came out to watch me in a sports game was when I was in Kilpatrick prison playing on the football team. My brother's family came.

That wasn't much to be proud about, but this was. I told everyone in my family I would be competing at Battle of the Bars. Their excitement about coming to see me replaced all of the nervousness and fear with joy. Tasha, Grandma Guera, my nephew Danny, and several of my cousins came.

I had been doing calisthenics for seven or eight months, but this was my first time at a fitness expo. I had no idea tens of thousands of people gathered at the L.A. Convention Center to watch two days of fitness competitions. My competition was on the second day. Most of my friends were competing on the first day so we all went down as a group to support each other.

The Fit Expo was a new world to me. Supplement companies, clothing companies, gyms – each had their own booths where women in bikinis and booty shorts handed out free samples. D.J. booths with lights and special effects blared music through large floor speakers. It was like a nightclub.

People waited in lines as long as those at Disneyland to take pictures with their favorite fitness celebrities. Some of these celebrities had millions of people following their lives on social media, which was foreign to me. Instagram was beginning to gain popularity, and I was still trying to figure that out. Ten years behind bars will set you back on technology.

Hanging from the ceiling were twenty-foot banners of muscle bound men flexing and beautiful women in bikinis. It was obvious that this wasn't just a hobby sport. This was a full-blown industry. I was trying to get into the mental head space that I needed to focus on the competition, which was difficult because of how star struck I was.

I was glad I did not have to compete until the following day. I was able to take in how exciting a spectacle this was. By the end of the day I had mellowed out, the shock and awe had worn off, and I was able to watch my friends compete. By day two, I was completely focused on the competition, and what I set out to do – win.

Despite my nerves, I was amped. I felt like when I went to prison for the first time. I was terrified of the unknown. I was scared I might die or be injured. But I was also stoked that I was in prison, the big league. I had been conditioned since I was in juvenile hall that the big time street thugs learn how to run and organize their gangs in prison. I could not wait to get in there. I had those same feelings that day at the Fit Expo. I was scared, but equally excited because this meant things were happening. I was finally doing something with my life that had real meaning.

We showed up a few hours before the competition and hung around. It is best to keep things as mellow as possible the morning of a competition. We had a good breakfast and walked around. I tried to relax and close my eyes for a few minutes.

Forty-five minutes before contest time, I stretched and got ready. I was listening to Tech N9ne on my headphones, trying to work up a sweat but to no avail. The convention center felt colder than it did the day before. My friends came to pump me up, reassuring me with words of encouragement.

The internal dialogue began, "It's now or never. It's just like prison – I'm either gonna live it and run it, or it's going to run me."

"This is real now. I lost my mom then lost my mind, but I found this. What are you gonna do with it? This isn't just some guys doing pull ups in a gym. This is the real thing. Time to prove yourself."

"What about that guy from Germany? He must be good. He must have money if he's flying all the way from Germany to compete. Fuck it, can't think about that. The time is right now. This is real, time to act."

The announcer runners came by to say they would be picking names to see who goes first. They announced over the convention center speakers that the contest was about to start. Coaches began their final preparations and gave their locker room speeches to their athletes. Crowds of people, herds of animals, moved to the stands behind the bars to watch. The hive was buzzing.

My energy level was off the charts. I was ready to go. I was amped but I remained calm and quiet, keeping my energy focused and precise.

I paced back and forth with my headphones on. I was wearing a T-shirt with my mom's picture on it. She must be here. She's the reason I'm here. Three guys went before me and then it was my turn. I took off the shirt and instinctively hung it on the bars as I walked on to the competition floor. I have done that in all my contests since. It made me feel as if she was in the front row watching me.

Thousands of people were in the crowd. I wasn't used to being the center of attention or on a stage, and honestly I didn't like it. I was still very institutionalized and shy. But I looked into the bleachers and saw my family. I looked behind me and saw my whole crew.

"All right, Mom. Watch this."

I held nothing back. I threw out high caliber maneuvers; it was all or nothing. I didn't hear or see anything. The crowd, the noise, the lights – it was all a deaf and blind blur. I was doing giant, swooping swings around the bars into backflip re-grabs. I laid it all out there. I was either going to destroy the competition, or I was going to let it destroy me.

I stuck every move. I had no doubt that I did the absolute best I could. "That's it. That's all I can do. Let's see where the chips fall," I said to my teammates as I walked off the gym floor. They were going crazy as if I already had won. I was so drained, physically and emotionally. I collapsed onto the bench with a winded smile and the satisfaction of total exertion.

The twelve guys after me finished their routines, and we waited for the judges to calculate the scores. Everyone was talking to their team about their runs, hyped from the round, but I was still in the zone.

I was grateful that this was my reality and tried to calm myself while I waited.

"Whatever happens – happens. But I know I killed that. I've gotten this far."

"My family is in the stands – I'm in a place that even has stands."

"I'm being judged for my skills, not being judged by a guy in a robe."

The judges were taking a long time with the tally and I was getting restless. My mind was talking to me, running random scenarios through my head. I had to move around and stay occupied. I'd take a lap around the convention center and check out the booths. Grab water from the concession stand. Talk to Tasha and my family

The announcer's voice boomed over the arena, louder than the D.J. booths, louder than the collective buzz of thousands of people in a single area.

"The Winner is...................... Chris "Tatted Strength" Luera!!!!"

The convention center erupted, and I searched the stands for my family. I saw my grandma Huera with her hands over her mouth and tears in her eyes. Tasha was smiling and clapping, and my cousins were giving each other hugs and high fives. I was flooded with a spectrum of emotions. Pure joy at what I had accomplished. Then a wobbling between being upset that my mother wasn't there and grateful that I was.

I went up to the podium to receive my trophy. It was what my mom had always wanted for me. She always told me that there was something out there for me. And here it was. An electric current swept through the crowd, bouncing off the walls of the arena. The applause and screams of joy blared from the stands, echoing around the Convention Center.

Bella Falconi – a top motivational speaker in the fitness world handed me that trophy – and it all became real. So real that I almost couldn't believe it. My life flashed before my eyes. Middle school, high school. The gangs and violence. Trying to make my mother proud. Not fitting in. All of these random snippets from the past twenty years passed through my head in rapid succession. All the questions that haunted me day and night: Was I a gang member? A criminal? An athlete? A drug baby with big dreams that weren't meant for me? All of that was wiped away. I was validated. When the woman handed me that trophy, she handed me my second life. I was reborn.

The trophy ceremony ended and I was exhausted physically and emotionally. I was in a fog. With so much going on around me, I felt like I was blowing in the wind. People were hugging each other and giving high fives. Strangers wanted to take pictures with me. It was surreal.

Grandma Huera, my sister-in-law's mother, put her ice cold hands on my face and pulled me close to her. She was so happy that she was crying, and she told me that my mother would have been proud of me. She had known my mother since they were little girls. They'd gone to high school together, grown up together, and eventually their kids married one another. They were lifelong best friends. Everybody was telling me how proud they were of me, but when she said it, that was the closest thing to hearing it from my mom. I had always wanted to make my mother proud – to accomplish something for her. When I got out of prison, stopped doing drugs, and stayed off the streets, my family was proud of me. But I didn't do anything to deserve that praise. I was just doing what regular people had been doing their entire lives. I stopped being a detriment to society and became neutral. There was no "accomplishment" in that.

But now, I finally had done something worthy of praise. I had poured my blood and sweat into the contest. I dedicated myself to the process, and saw it through to the end. I put in the work to achieve this victory, and to have my family validate that was sweeter than the victory itself.

Walking out of the L.A. Convention Center I felt a new emotion– empowerment. Not only am I going to do this forever, no one can stop me.

Chapter Ten

I now hoped to give back the joy fitness gave me to others. After mastering all the techniques from Kenneth's class, I asked him if he could show me how to teach the material.

I quit my job at the catering company and became a personal trainer and teacher of Ken's class where I once was a student. I was feeling fulfilled at work and took pride in the responsibility I had to my students and clients. Every so often, I would take a step back, a deep breath, and look at the trajectory of my life. Looking back at my gang and drug years was like watching a movie of somebody else's life.

After I won the Battle of the Bars, my popularity rose. People wanted to train with me. When the crew and I would go to Venice Beach, random people came up to me either to show me love, or ask me about my workout routines. I grew a decent following on social media of people that wanted an inside look at my life. People were paying attention to the positive things I was contributing. I didn't even know how to use social media well. When I got out of prison I had a flip phone and never caught up on technology.

I picked up clients, an additional class to teach, and enjoyed the ride. A few months later, Zach, who I competed against, reached out to our crew about a contest he was holding in his outdoor backyard gym at his house in Florida. I loved the butterflies in my stomach when I knew I could go home and tell my family about another competition. Seeing the smiles on their faces and the light in their eyes was always more important than the competition itself. I got the most joy from telling my father and sister that I was going to travel to compete. That was winning for me; the contest was a bonus.

We flew out to the competition in October, landing in the middle of a tropical weather cell, a storm system that brings warm water from the Caribbean and mixes it with cooler air from the north Atlantic. The result was a lot of rain. I arrived at Zach's house to find the competition in a state of chaos. Competitors were backing out because of the rain, either unwilling to compete in the poor weather, or not able to get to Florida because of it. The tournament was now much smaller than planned. Zach and I made it to the finals with little challenge, and battled each other for the championship.

I warmed up for the finals, but I didn't feel right. The weather was getting to my head, and my lack of contest experience showed. I voiced my doubts to Justin about being able to do my routine in the rain. He gave me the usual locker room speech and told me I'd be fine.

I made no adjustments for the weather and went right into my final routine. My first trick wasa Fly-Away Leshay, which is a back flip from one bar onto another bar. I came down through the rotation to grab the bar, but I slipped off the wet steel and landed on my back. I was frustrated and picked myself up, and that is where I made my critical mistake. I allowed that fail to bother me. Instead of modifying my routine, I wanted to go bigger to make up for the miss.

I jumped, grabbed the bar, and began swinging, setting up my next trick. I went into a backflip re-grab – my signature move. I was one of only three guys doing it at that time. Again, I came through the air, saw the bar, went to grab it, and slipped off.

***

That trip to Florida was important for two reasons. First, although I lost the competition, I gained valuable, battle tested experience. Second, I met Ed Checo, founder of Barstarzz, a calisthenics team out of New York City. Ed was one of the judges for the competition, and I immediately recognized him when I got to Zach's. I had been watching Barstarzz videos on YouTube since I began calisthenics.

Ed came up to me after the competition. "The weather sucks, but you were doing some crazy shit, man. Keep doing what you're doing. The Street Workout Federation is having a world championship in Moscow, and they need two U.S. representatives. You should try out." He said to me.

The Street Workout Federation held a contest to decide who the two representatives would be. The contest was an online video submission, where you would post a two-minute video of your best routine. Ed told me the rules and was adamant that I submit.

I was caught off guard; I didn't know what to say. It was a great compliment just to be considered good enough to try out. I was star struck by the whole situation. Ed talking to me, competitions, being accepted and complimented by people I idolized– I was both amazed and bewildered by all of it. Romanticized dreams of the future danced around my head on the flight home. I thought about having the opportunity to compete against the best guys in the world, people that I learned from. A fire to compete in a world competition was ignited.

The following week, I had a client film my routine on the bars at Venice Beach, and I sent it off. Time went by and I continued to train and teach. My following gained momentum and everyone in the calisthenics scene in L.A. knew who I was. It was an exciting time. I couldn't believe that people were looking up to me. I almost forgot about the video.

A month or so later I got a call from Ed. "You won, man! You're going to represent the United States in the world championships in Moscow. Congratulations."

I was floored. I screamed as loud as I could with joy and drove straight to my father's house. I barreled through the front door. "Dad! I won! I won that contest. I am going to represent the United States and I'm flying to Moscow to compete."

My father couldn't move well from a bad hip, but jumped out of his chair. "Wow. That is something," he said over and over again.

In that moment I knew I had already won. I won my way into the competition, and now I was playing with house money. I'm a convicted felon who can't even vote in the United States. Yet I was chosen to represent my country in an international competition. It was an honor. I had never even been outside the country.

The flight from Los Angeles to Moscow was twelve hours. When I arrived, I was so excited that I could have come in last and it wouldn't have mattered.

That mindset was a successful one. It kept me calm and fluid, detached from expectations and results. It allowed me to compete freely and relaxed. In the forefront of my mind, ahead of the competition itself, was the honor I was given and the opportunity I had earned to represent the United States.

The competition was held in an outdoor arena in the middle of Moscow. There were BMX contests, basketball tournaments, and at night a big concert party. The calisthenics competition was held in the late afternoon – one of the headline events – and there were men from sixty five countries competing.

I sat in the hot summer sun waiting for my turn, jittery with nerves. I finally heard my name announced and a shot of adrenaline bolted through my body like it was completing an electrical circuit.

I went up to the bar flying with energy and went through my two-minute routine. I was not even thinking about my next move. I performed off pure muscle memory and the rush of adrenaline. To end my set, I stood on the parallel bars and did a high, swooping backflip off them. I overshot the backflip and landed on top of one of the judges. The crowd roared. They loved it. I left the stage happy with my performance and went to the chill zone where the other athletes awaited the end of the round.

As I watched the next few competitors, people congratulated me on my performance. One of them was Rain Bennett, a filmmaker. He passed me and said as he passed by, "You killed it, get ready for your next round." He didn't even wait for me to answer – he just said that and walked away. The top fifteen competitors would make it to the second round, and I didn't think I would be amongst them. I had no expectation of actually doing well, and his comment confused me.

I watched the rest of the heat and listened for the judges to announce the top fifteen. To my utter astonishment, they called my name. I was already doing better than I had ever anticipated. I had nothing to lose.

I went a little too big to start the second round. I went for a Fly Away Leshay. I slipped off the second bar and landed square on my back. First move of the round, and I botched it. I hopped right up and shook it off. The fall jarred something loose in my memory, and I remembered my competition in Florida where I failed because I kept trying the same move. That mindset is a crapshoot. If you try the same move and stick it, people love you for it. If you keep trying and fail, you look foolish for not moving on. I chose to move on and finished my set.

I came off the stage feeling better than when I walked into the competition. The fact I made the finals meant that I was among the top fifteen in the world. That was good enough for me. I went back to the chill zone and relaxed. Again I saw Rain approaching me with his camera. He began filming me, saying, "Are you ready for the podium?"

I didn't understand what was up with this guy. "I'm just out here trying to do my best. Just happy to be here," I replied, annoyed.

He told me to get ready for the podium.

The heat finished and we waited while the six judges conferred and did their scoring. I just wanted third place.

A booming voice came over the loudspeaker, "In third place Robert Polansky of Latvia!" The crowd erupted and the rest of competitors gave him applause. "In second place, Chris Luera of the United States!" The crowd exploded again. The shouting and applause was almost deafening. For a moment I forgot where I was. It felt like a dream. I couldn't believe this was my life. This was the fruit of my hard work and determination. My dream had become reality.

"First place Eric Ortiz of France!"

As I took to the podium, the atmosphere was surreal. Tasha was crying out with joy. I could feel her energy from across the arena. The trophy girl came over to put a medal around my neck and all I could do was thank her repeatedly. She looked like I was freaking her out a bit but I was ecstatic.

After the ceremony, everyone was mingling amongst a buzz of conversation. Disappointment was worn on the faces of those who didn't place, and elation on those who did. People were coming up to me to take pictures. Kids ran up and wanted my shirt. One even wanted to take home my shoes. The only thing on my mind was getting to a phone and calling my dad.

I grabbed Tasha and we went back to the hotel where I called my father and Toni. I told him I placed second out of sixty-five countries, and they told me they were proud of me. It meant more to me to hear that than any trophy or accolade I would receive, or anything else that would eventually come from this.

***

Placing in the world championships was important for my career because it automatically qualified me for the second big event the Street Workout Federation holds – the Superfinals, which was being held in Norway. Qualifiers from all over the world competed for a spot. I had not even left Russia, and I found out I would be traveling to Norway to compete later in the year.

Thinking about the journey I was on, made me well up with tears; I just could not believe it – it was too surreal. I'd spiraled downward, to the pits of demoralization, then up a beautiful, winding road of freedom and joy. The prison bars kept me locked in. The calisthenics bars set me free.

I tapped into a well of gratitude and positivity that I never thought was available to me, but it wasn't without its lining of sadness. I was upset my mom wasn't here to witness how good things had become. She couldn't see the transformation my life had undergone and the energy that now carried it – which was on a much higher wavelength.

In the hotel room in Russia, I realized what all of us realize at some point in our lives – that our parents were right all along. I fought my mother every step of the way about everything – drugs, gangs, what to do with my life. I was hardheaded and would not listen to her advice. All along she was right, and it took me multiple trips to prison to realize it. In that time, I lost many moments I could have spent with her. But had I not walked down the path I did, I wouldn't be where I am today. My mother believed in me when nobody, not even I, believed in me. She told me this would happen, all I had to do was work for it.

Then it hit me, like the sky cleared all at once and I could finally see. She was with me this whole time. She did see my transformation. I thought back to the day Ace reached his hand out to me in MetroFlex. That moment was the genesis of my new life. I never would have stuck my hand out and introduced myself to him. I know with conviction that my mother's spirit was responsible for that, and everything since. I was now traveling the world, doing what I love, with the person who means the most to me – my beautiful wife Tasha.

Before Norway, I was a celebrity judge at a competition in New York City. The winner in New York would qualify for Norway. When we landed in Norway, I had quite a bit of culture shock. Their culture was far removed from the one I was used to in the United States; it was safe. Tasha and I had severe jetlag from the time change, and we went for walks at night to kill time. We approached the bellboy in the lobby, and I fired off questions at him.

"How's the neighborhood?"

"Is it safe to walk around at night?"

"Is What neighborhood's should we avoid?"

He looked at me like I had walked in from another dimension.

"This is Norway, you have nothing to worry about," he replied.

I felt a bit ignorant, but I was supposed to be in a prison cell, not exploring foreign countries. We walked around the waterfront, on beautiful cobblestone streets, laughing and joking, as we got lost through the snaking turns of the city. It was like when we first met. Half delirious with exhaustion, we floated into the early hours of the morning until we stumbled, stomachs aching from laughter, into our hotel room to sleep.

***

My experience in the Superfinals humbled me and made me understand what it means to be an athlete. The competition was fun, and the set up was great. There was a stage with the bar equipment on it, surrounded by bleachers. Spotlights from the ceiling lit up the stage, while the audience was blacked out. I performed well. My routine went just how I planned. But I came up short. I finished in ninth place. I felt like a little kid who studied all night for the test and still failed.

Being an international athlete, I realized that I am not going to feel at the top of my game all the time. There are just too many factors: time zone changes, jet lag, weather and climate changes, kinks and aches from the flight. I had to learn to account for, and adapt to, all of these variables. The SuperFinals exposed my weaknesses and flaws, which I could work on remedying.

When you are winning, you ride a wave of energy that pushes you to train harder. After a mediocre performance, the competitive fire inside burns even hotter fueled by the disappointment of not winning. That is when the tenacity to take it to the next level really comes alive. The best motivator I have used for my training is mediocrity and the willingness to do anything to avoid it. I had to learn – through trial by fire – that being an athlete means losing and bouncing back. It means fighting through adversity. There is always going to be another competition, and it's always time to start training for the next contest.

And that's what I did. I got back in the gym, and got busy. I continued to train and competed in the World Calisthenics Organization. I won, and became the middleweight world champion.

After my first world championship, competitions, trainings, and seminars were regular occurrences. I was constantly in the gym or on the road. I received an invitation to Kazakhstan to represent the United States in another international competition. I competed at my heaviest ever – 198 pounds. I won the Best Style competition and came in fourth overall. When I returned, I was almost immediately on the road to Las Vegas to defend my middleweight championship. I won my second world championship.

Next was Germany, where I received my first head-to-head loss to a guy from London, who is now a good friend of mine, named Sensei. The rigorous traveling and competition schedule was wearing on my body, and I went into the contest slightly injured. I had aggravated a longtime back problem. Losing a head-to-head for the first time was a setback. After my two world titles, it gave me some necessary humility. My life blew up quick. One day I was a nobody working out at the bars on

Venice Beach, and not even a year later I was two-time world champion. I was a personal trainer and teacher. People were traveling from all over the world to train with my crew and me. I felt invincible – untouchable. I needed that loss to put my ego in check. It motivated me to get back in the gym and train harder. Eventually, I got a rematch with Sensei in Birmingham, England. I won the contest and with it, my third world championship.

Chris Luera: Ex-gang member, ex-felon, ex-drug addict – current three-time WCO world champion. Who I was, is just as much a part of me, as who I am. In the beginning, my motivation came from the fear of never wanting to become those things again. As I slipped deeper into desperation after my mother died, I almost went back there. Fear snapped me out, but love made me stay. Fear is a great motivator, but only temporarily. Sooner or later you forget what you are afraid of. It has to transform into something else – love.

I found that love in the sport of calisthenics. Bars, the defining symbol of my entrapment, became my vessel towards freedom and my ticket to a new life. It gave me the means to travel the world, experience different places, and meet people that I never would have been able to on my own accord.

In between my competitions I became a trainer and coach for the World Calisthenics Organization. As their middleweight champion, I was one of their premier athletes, which afforded me the opportunity to travel and teach their workshops.

In the winter of 2014 the WCO held a week-day workshop in Dubai. It was a big success. One of the clients, a man named Yousuf, owned a local gym in Dubai called Gravity. Yousuf took one of Ken's workshops a year ago, and loved it so much that he opened up a gym. Yousuf is one of the most laid back people I have ever met. He's a quiet guy but he's a cobra, striking quick and precise out of nowhere. He is also brilliant, one of the smartest men I have ever met. As he was opening Gravity, he was getting his Master's degree in architecture. He was doing all of this at the age of twenty-six. Our workshop went so well that Yousuf asked me to stay in Dubai and work for him at Gravity. I was honored. I had always dreamt of living in a foreign country, but I have never lived more than a few blocks from where I grew up, except when I went to prison, so I didn't seriously consider it.

I loved Dubai. Before I went, I watched too many news broadcasts and watched too many movies about the Middle East, and they gave me a false perspective on where I was going. When I got there it was completely different than anything I had seen. It was beautiful. The society itself was fascinating to me. It is a progressive culture. Crime levels are low. You could forget your backpack at the food court, and it would be there when you got back. They preach equality, and they consistently innovate in renewable energy. The vibes of the conversations with people were much different than America. People were talking about starting their own business, or how to make their business better. Whatever the topic is, the conversation always seems to be centered on improving the lives of people – even the newspaper prints positive stories.

I had a perception change that first trip to Dubai, and fell in love with the city and the culture. And the money. I had never been around so much wealth in my life. A few months later Yousuf called me and asked me again to come and work for him. This time it was not just a comment in passing. He was not going to get off the phone with me until I agreed to come work at his gym.

"Now I'm getting asked to move across the world?" I thought. I thanked him and said I had to talk it over with my wife and father. The thought of breaking that mold of our close family and being the first to leave San Pedro was a source of fear for me. My father and sister were as surprised as I was, and I could hear the same kind of fear in their voices that I was feeling in myself. At first, the plan was to move there for a couple of years. My father and sister were happy for me, but they didn't like the idea. Could I blame them? I had spent nearly all of my adult life in prison, now I came home and finally found my path in life, only to leave. And it wasn't like I was moving within the United States. I'm moving across the globe to the Middle East.

I went back to Yousuf and told him that I couldn't make it happen. I couldn't leave my father, sister, and family back in San Pedro. He was relentless. He told me just to try it for four or five months – nothing permanent. I could sell four or five months to my folks. They bought into that idea. When I got my family's blessing is when the real fear and anxiety kicked in. Am I really about to do this? Do I even deserve this? I was terrified of stepping outside the tiny box of San Pedro that I had known my entire life. Before moving to Dubai, I went through periods of extreme self-doubt. I beat myself up for leaving – abandoning the family. Another part of me didn't think I deserved such an amazing opportunity because of what I had done in the past.

On top of this I was a nervous about moving to another country. Going into prison was scary because of the fear of the unknown, but there was no fear of failure element to it. I had already failed. Prison was the end of the line. But when I was given the opportunity to go to a foreign country and teach fitness, I felt the pressure and fear of potential failure.

That fear of failure had held me back my entire life. It was the reason I never applied myself in school. One of my prison tattoos says "Fuck what you think" across my chest. But in reality, I care a lot about what you think. I'm terrified to fail because of how it will make me look. I was dominated by fear and self-loathing, and they were the reasons for many of the choices I made. Several years out of prison, a new life, and three world championships later, those ghosts of the past were still hanging around in the deep recesses of my subconscious. Even with the probability of success in Dubai, fear of failure whispered to me its conjured up stories of all the ways this could go wrong.

Larger than that fear, however, was the responsibility I had to this career and the commitment I made to this life. When I was engaged in the mental debate over whether to go, Tasha's light cut through the fog and guided me back to safe shores. I would come home from a workout or teaching a class, and talk to her about what was going on in between my ears. I'd voice my fears, excitement, and anxiety. She would patiently listen, then chime in with simple words of encouragement.

Tasha couldn't move to Dubai with me. She was pursuing her own career in teaching and had to stay in San Pedro to teach and go to school. We had many conversations preceding my move to Dubai.

She said, "You have to go. You have this opportunity, take it. You put a lot of time and effort into all of this, and you loved Dubai when you were there for the workshop. You didn't stop talking about how beautiful it was. Why not do it? You have to."

She was right. I couldn't shy away from this. Without her I am not certain I would have gone, or if I'd even be in the position I am today. She has always been supportive of my career and me. Even when I quit my catering job to pursue fitness full time, she was behind me. When faced with a husband saying, "I quit my job, and I'm gonna do this. I'm going to chase this dream," most women would've asked "what do you mean THIS, and how is THIS going to pay the bills? Where is the money going to come from?" It was never like that with Tasha. Her gentle wisdom allowed me to be free to chase my dream. I had just as much of a responsibility to her to catch it.

I tuned out the voices in my head and channeled the voices of Tasha and my mother. I pressed on. I made my decision and I was going to stick to it. I owed it to my wife, my family, and myself, and even if I failed, I could rest easier knowing I tried my best. It turned out to be one of the most life altering experiences I've had. It was a new well of personal growth.

Chapter Eleven

Success through hard work. It is a Luera family principle – an American principle – and I was living it. In the weeks preceding my departure, I was coordinating the details of my stay with Yousuf and Mico, the gym managers. I wanted to know every detail. They exhibited a lot of patience with me those few weeks. I was expecting a major culture clash between my blue-collar Los Angeles gang upbringing and this wealthy Middle Eastern culture. I was overthinking every detail, and planning for the worst, but I found that my fear of a culture clash was much greater than what I experienced.

I left for Dubai in November 2015. It was an Indian summer, and unusually hot for six-thirty on a fall morning. I barely slept the night before, as my mind decided to run through every possible scenario of what could happen. Fame and fortune, bitter failure, a trip back to prison, and the plane crashing before I even arrived in Dubai, bounced like a pinball through the machine of my mind. Some fantasies were fun to play with for a while, and I'd indulge in their lavishness. Others were so bad that I'd lie staring at the ceiling for a half hour trying to think my way out of it. I eventually wore myself out through mental exhaustion. I was able to get a few hours of sleep.

At four a.m. the alarm went off. I was already awake and roaring around by the time Tasha rolled over. She took a look at the tornado that was ripping through the bedroom, and pulled the sheets back over her head. I checked my bag at least four times for underwear, my toothbrush, and passport. As I tore through the house, throwing clothes, books, and fitness gear all about, Tasha calmly got out of bed, got dressed, made coffee, and slipped my plane tickets, which I had forgotten – into my backpack. I gulped down a cup of coffee, and was out the door. When we got to LAX I pulled the luggage out of the trunk and kissed my wife goodbye.

Before I arrived in Dubai, I stopped in England for a workshop in Birmingham. From there I flew into Dubai International Airport. I slept most of the flight, and was grateful for it, as it was the only real rest I had in several days. The combination of training and jetlag was taking a toll on my body. Flights always tightened up my back.

As we descended into Dubai, it was as magical as the first time I saw it. We came in over the sea, a blank expanse that covered hundreds of miles until the shoreline appeared. Then it was sand for another twenty minutes, until a city emerged out of the emptiness of desert. The Burj Al-Arab and Burj Khalifa – the world's tallest building – reached for the sky as the rest of the city huddled around it like a hive. It was an experience just to fly into – one moment you are in one of the most remote corners of the world, and the next a metropolis blooms in front of your eyes. The plane landed and several people clapped for the pilot.

Dubai in November is a beautiful time of the year, probably the best time to travel there. It is not too hot, and the temperature settles between seventy-five to ninety degrees during the day with no humidity. Ken, my friend, teacher, and mentor, was going to be teaching with me at Gravity gym. He had already been working there for a month before I arrived, and I was going to stay for several weeks after he left. He had been renting a room in someone's house and just moved into the apartment we would share for the next five months. I had one thing on my mind – get to Ken.

Yousuf picked me up from the airport and took me to the apartment. He must have moved in only a few days ago because it was largely empty– no television, no Wi-Fi, just beds and a couch.

"You need to message anyone?" Yousuf said.

He connected me to a hotspot he created using his phone, and I sent messages to my sister, father, and wife, letting them know I landed and loved them.

"Cool, man. I gotta run back to the gym. I'll be back to pick you up and take you there in a couple of hours, but get some rest first, you must be exhausted," Yousuf said.

It was like being a kid and watching your mother – your only lifeline – leave the room. "Where are you going?! You can't just leave me here!" I wanted to say. "Thanks for your hospitality brother, can't wait. I'll see you soon" is what I did say with a smile. And then I was alone.

"Whaaaaaat the fuck. did you just get yourself in too? You just moved across the world for half a year. You really went off the deep end this time. What are you thinking? You know you're gonna fail right? You're gonna blow it. You're gonna walk into the gym to teach your first class and everyone is going to say 'What is this stupid American going to teach me. What's that tattooed on him? He has tattoos... on his head?'"

There was nothing to distract me, or take my mind off of my thoughts. I had to sit with these hideous feelings. Looking back on that moment in the apartment from where I am now, I was more anxious being in Dubai than I was about being in a prison cell. That fear of failure is a strong emotion; it will make a coward out of any man. There is only one way to go when faced with fear – straight through it. Trying to avoid it will only destroy you. Fear is the great defeater of success, and somewhere there is a graveyard of dreams, all casualties of that monster.

I soon blacked out from the exhaustion of traveling, and woke up to Yousuf pounding on the door. The sound startled me awake, and for a moment I didn't know where I was. I greeted Yousuf at the door. He said, "Hey brother, you ready to go check out the gym? Ken should be done with his class by the time we get there." I threw on some clothes.

As we drove through the streets of Dubai, I absorbed my new home. It was sunny – eighty-five degrees – the streets were lined with palm trees and skyscrapers of glass and steel. The city was a shining gem of man-made wealth. The blacks and dark blues of the buildings reflected the sun down onto the streets, which bustled with Arab and Caucasian businessmen rushing to work. Exotic cars – Lamborghinis, Ferraris, and Bentleys – with custom paint jobs slithered through the morning traffic. Yousuf had Tupac playing on the radio, and I thought for a moment I was in a music video, I had no other frame of reference for what I was experiencing.

At Gravity there was not a single exercise or treadmill machine. The entire gym was devoted to the sport of calisthenics. In the center of the gym was a large structure that looked like a piece of playground equipment on steroids. There were two pull up bars on each end with lateral bars connecting them. There was a row of stand alone pull up bars on one end, and a set of parallel bars on the other. Scattered throughout the gym were different mats, box jumps, and free weights of all shapes and sizes. Rows of potted plants surrounded the gym floor, and on the far wall, a large sign said "gravity" in grass. The gym was state of the art with brand new equipment.

The front desk staff greeted me with an embracing welcome. Everybody was smiling, and people stopped what they were doing to introduce themselves. I was so grateful. I had traveled half way across the world, not sure what I was getting myself into. What I needed was the love these people showed me. That went a long way to making me feel welcomed. A sense of accomplishment and pride came over me. The crazy monkey chatter of my brain subsided, and a calm, but strong, purpose came over me. It was my first breath of serenity in the long weeks that led up to this moment.

I put my bag down outside the gym floor and as soon as I picked my head up, I saw Ken coming towards me with a big smile and open arms.

"What's up, man? So good to see you," he said, hugging me.

He had just finished teaching a class and had the rest of the day free. The rest of the morning we worked out, and grabbed lunch with a few of the other trainers. At day's end we went back to the apartment. I was physically and emotionally drained, but finally I was in a good place. My head was clear – for the most part. I was still worried if the clients would like the class I was teaching, but the anxiety came and went. Everything was working out.

The class I was going to teach – a general introduction to calisthenics and body weight exercises – started in two days. To prepare for it, I did what I always do – watch Ken. Growing up I bought into the "self-made man" concept that society shoves down our throats. The one that tells us we have to make it on our own and never ask for help. Calisthenics showed me that concept is false. I learned everything I know from other people. Other people who have attained success were taught everything they know from other successful people. That's the natural order of things, and anyone who has achieved anything in life will tell you that you need people to get where you want to go. So I watched Ken. I observed how he taught the class and interacted with the clients. Then I'd put my own spin on it with my personality. That is how it has always been for me. Watch, listen, and learn.

The days were spent going to Ken's morning class, then getting a workout. We'd break for lunch, then I'd come back to the gym in the afternoon and watch how the gym itself operated. My main concern for those two days was getting comfortable with my environment.

To my surprise, and relief, Dubai is very similar to many of the western countries I had been to. In fact, it was much more like America than Europe. They drove on the right side of the road, and most of their driving laws are the same as ours. The biggest difference was their aggressive driving. I've been to places with highly aggressive drivers, specifically Russia, and even being from Los Angeles I am used to crazy drivers. But the people in Dubai were by far the worst. The worst cutting off in Los Angeles would be considered courteous in Dubai. They are maniacal behind the wheel.

The hustle also stuck out for me. Everyone in Dubai was hustling and grinding, and there was a ton of money to show for it. I saw virtually no signs of unemployment; everybody was making money. In Los Angeles, we have a lot of homeless people, as well as people who are not working. But even the people who work are working towards not working one day. Dubai was like the pilgrimage that every hustler in the world was destined to make. Even at the gym, the Parkour trainer was from India, another trainer was from Ukraine. Mico and the front desk staff were from the Philippines. We were all there to make money. That was inspirational for me, and I had a lot of respect for the mindset I was witnessing. It was beautiful to be a part of. Everyone in this city was putting in work and growing. I was doing the same thing. I was a part of this buzzing energy of people all trying to make a better life – people who were leaving their past lives and countries, who had traveled here to make something of their lives. I began to look at everything through the lenses of growth and inspiration.

Two days later I taught my first class. I walked into the gym at nine sharp. As I stretched and warmed up, clients of all kinds trickled in. We had the college frat boys in their cutoff t-shirts, the stay at home mom dressed in neon from head to toe, the business man getting in his morning workout before the day started. It was a variety of people at different points in their fitness program. I introduced myself to everyone.

We had about twenty clients for the first class. The only time I felt nervous was when we started. I got up in the front of the room, and saw twenty sets of focused eyes staring at me, waiting on my direction. Over the past year, I had grown more comfortable speaking in front of people. I used to freeze I was so terrified. Like not able to speak or move, kind of terrified. But a few months prior, I attended a public speaking program called Toastmasters to get better at public speaking. When I stood in front of that fitness class, I was thankful for that program. It made me much more comfortable speaking in front of people.

After we got into the workouts, it seemed like the hour-long class flashed by. It was a success. The students loved the class, and me. I was the "new trainer from America," interesting and edgy, polite and reserved. At least those were the reviews I got.

After that first week, I thawed out and relaxed. I wasn't plagued by nervousness or worry. I felt like I was in a groove. I was at peace again.

***

Everyone I knew in Dubai was through the gym. A tight knit group, we treated each other like family. From the owners to the front desk staff, everyone was equal. It was a pleasure to work in such a friendly environment. After a month or so, I settled into a routine and immersed myself in the local culture with help of clients and trainers.

Ken and I were like superstars to our clients. One of them invited a large group of us out to dinner at the Burj-Al Arab, the world's only seven-star hotel. Ken and I didn't know much about it, until we pulled up to a line of exotic cars with men in tuxedos and women in ballroom gowns hopping out of them. We were wearing T-shirt and jeans. The parking valet looked at us half puzzled, half insulted.

Our friend, a client, greeted us warmly. As we walked through the lobby, a labyrinth of yellow and blue marble unraveled in front of us and thirty-foot gold pillars stretched to the ceiling. People looked us with judging eyes until they saw who we were with. I didn't know at the time, how well connected our hosts were. Unbeknownst to us we were guests of royalty. When we sat down for dinner, I looked around at the lavish display of wealth. I could not help but to start laughing. It was unbelievable. I could not wrap my head around the fact that this was real. I gripped the armrests of the chair to make sure.

The walls were adorned with gold. Silk cloths decorated the tables and crown molding with coffered ceilings enclosed us in a cocoon of elegance. I peeked at the menu. Some items bore four-digit prices. I had never seen anything like this before in my life – not even in a movie. It was beyond what I could have imagined existed. This was a new world – a new culture, and I did not know this guy who brought us here, but I knew he was important. This was important. At one point in my life I was convinced I'd never make it out of a six by eight concrete prison cell. I thought about my old homies I used to gangbang with. If I ran in to them on the street and told them I was just in Dubai, they would probably ask me what a "Dubai" is. I thought about my mom. A wave of gratitude came over me.

As my time in Dubai went on, I grew comfortable with my new life. I was making good money – more money than I ever legally made– and proved myself as an asset to the gym. Every day my schedule was packed from 5 a.m. to 7 p.m. teaching fitness classes. On top of that, I had four private personal training clients. At night, we would go out to a club, or eat at a nice restaurant, and enjoy the nightlife. It was a smooth, beautiful time when everything came easy. The experience was also one of deep, powerful growth. Every day I was making life-changing memories, experiencing things that people only get to do on vacation. Dinners at five star restaurants, hiking, or skydiving over the Palm Islands were our typical recreational activities.

In the great timeline of a human life, a few months are generally an insignificant period of time, merely a small point on the map. But this time in Dubai was concentrated with more growth for me as a human being than decades of my life.

The ten years I spent going in and out of prison, committing crimes, and before that in my childhood; even as a kid in middle school stealing candy to sell on the schoolyard for extra money, the culmination of it all meant I never grew as a man. A tree will grow into the pot you plant it. A tree in a small pot can only grow so much; its roots can only go so deep. If that tree was placed into the ground, free of its limitations, it will grow to its full potential. A prison cell was my pot. Equally as devastating to my growth was the prison cell of my mind. The one in which I told myself I had no value, had nothing to contribute to society, that I would be a failure relegated to a life of crime. That mental prison is much harder to break free from. I still sometimes go back to it even to this day.

In the seven years since I was released from prison, I experienced more growth than in my entire previous life. Getting off drugs, staying away from the streets, and finally getting off parole were all small battles that I won. They were stepping stones along the way of the Great Path. They all led me to this moment, where for the first time in my life I felt like I was taken out of the pot and all its constraints – mental and material – and placed into the ground. There is no limit to how deep my roots can grow or how high I can reach.

The five months in Dubai went by quickly, and towards the end, I was excited to return to Los Angeles. I wanted to see Tasha and my dad. My experience in Dubai changed my perception of the world and my life. I was excited to share my experience, growth, and success with the two people I loved the most. I was also sad to leave the people I had grown so close to. Yousef, Mico, and all of the staff at Gravity had become family to me. They took care of me and gave me a lot of love.

I was growing in financial success, as well. My personal training business was getting bigger and word was spreading about my skill. Job opportunities for me in Los Angeles were much thinner. Dubai is relatively small, but if you are a good trainer, you can do very well. Los Angeles, on the other hand, is the global capital of physical fitness. Everyone, it seems, is a yoga instructor, personal trainer, or nutritionist. If you aren't a big name, training athletes and stars, or if you don't have the capital to open up your own gym, it can be tough to get by. The attitude towards fitness is much different in Los Angeles. People either don't care about fitness, or they are very snobby about it, and only go to the most glamorous trainers and gyms. They want all the bells and whistles, most of which have nothing to do with the craft of fitness.

Yousuf and Mico wanted me to stay. For weeks before I left, at least once a week, they would make me an offer. I told them I loved them, and I was grateful for the opportunity, but I had to return to Los Angeles and my family. Tasha and my dad are my world, and I could not act out in my own self-interest and stay in Dubai, dragging Tasha there with me, and not being home for my father. I had to go home, but I looked forward to returning to

Dubai. I still look forward to that day. When times get hard in Los Angeles, I fantasize about moving back to Dubai. Maybe someday, when things are right and circumstances change.

The staff at Gravity held a going away party for me at the Cheesecake Factory. We had bonded over the past five months, and traded story after story for hours into the night, until the waitstaff checked on us every ten minutes, the subtle hint that they wanted to close. In the morning Yousuf drove me to the airport. The flight home was a push and pull between being ecstatic to see my father and Tasha and missing Dubai. Eventually my excitement to see my family won. Gangs and prison felt like a lifetime ago – a distant, hazy memory that felt foreign to me, like another person lived it, and I was just a spectator. My physical appearance was the first to change after prison, but now my state of mind had undergone a full metamorphosis. I had shed my old self and was transformed.

Chapter Twelve

My flight connected in Doha, Qatar, and from there it was a fourteen-hour trip to Los Angeles. To make these long flights bearable, I came up with a ritual: The night before a flight I stay up all night, watching TV, bad re-runs, 1970s war movies, whatever comes on just to keep myself awake. In the morning, I drink bottomless cups of coffee to keep myself functional. By the time we pull up to the airport I am a zombie with a single-track mind – get in my plane seat. I push through security, the gates, and onto the plane. Once I am on the plane I stay up as long as I can. I watch the in-flight movies. If I read, I will be asleep instantly. Once my body has had enough, and my eyelids close on their own, I go to sleep. If I do this right, I can make it through flights of ten or more hours asleep most of the time.

When I landed in Los Angeles, my friend and lawyer David Pisarra picked me up. It was midday in August, and the smell of warm asphalt and traffic hit me in the nose when I walked out of the airport. I had slept during the flight, but I was groggy. I felt like I was in a dream and I just shuffled myself into the car. Dave dropped me off in San Pedro, where my father, sister, and Tasha were waiting for me.

I walked in the door to shouts of excitement. I barely got through the threshold, when Tasha pounced on me with an embrace. She kissed and hugged me so hard that she almost choked the wind out of me. My sister and father did the same. They wanted to hear all about the trip.

As I ran through the highlight reel of my trip, I got lost in these stories I was sharing. Occasionally I would break out of it and catch a glimpse of the amazement and wonder on their faces. These experiences were as much a part of me as jail and gangs. I owned all of it. I was still in awe that I was not in prison, and that I had traveled all over the world and had even lived in another country. I began to wonder if I could share that hope and experience with others.

I gave up on myself at fourteen years old. I had been in juvenile hall four or five times by then. My biological parents were both drug addicts and criminals. I thought that it was in my genetic make-up to follow in their footsteps. I thought I was predestined to be a loser, and so I gave up on myself early in life. For so long – many years of my life – I was stuck. Change was not possible. I proved myself wrong. Not only is change possible, but success is as well. I am also in a position to help other people, and I feel a responsibility to do so.

My life in Los Angeles fell back into its groove fairly quickly. During the week I trained clients, and on the weekends, the crew and I worked out at Venice or Santa Monica beach. I was not working as much as I was in Dubai and that bummed me out for a bit. Over there I had five clients a day every day, and when I got home I had five a week. But I began to build my brand – Tatted Strength. My social media swelled to over one hundred and fifty thousand followers. People from all over the world wanted to get a glimpse into my life. I made short clips, tutorials, and training videos and created a logo and had some T-shirts made. From that, the Tatted Strength brand was born.

The philosophy behind the name Tatted Strength is strength and perseverance. Calisthenics is who I am, and I made the decision to devote my life to the sport. For me, it is permanent like a tattoo. The sport made me not only physically strong, but mentally and emotionally, as well. It lifted me up out of the belly of hell and pushed me forward. It brought positivity to my life that I never thought possible, and a strength that will last forever. I want it to be a brand to inspire people to find what gives them strength, and to tap into the inner strength that lives within us all. It can be used to overcome all of life's trials. Tatted Strength is a statement that I am strong and will forever be strong.

I also had plans to take my story to the world. I knew my story could help people. In 2016 my lawyer Dave, a short attorney with eclectic interests from Santa Monica, came up with the idea to do a book about my life. We kicked the idea around and a few months later I began working on this book with writer Mike Oropollo.

At the same time I was traveling internationally to teach calisthenics and share my story. Over six months I went to Guatemala, England, and Dubai. The trip to Dubai was a two-day fitness expo where I was hired to teach and speak. The first day I taught a full calisthenics class and the second day was an inspirational speech I gave about my life. Afterward, people told me how motivational my story was. Most people couldn't believe I was still alive. They said, "You need to share this with the world." "Kids have to hear your story." They reinforced the idea that was rattling in my head for months – I need to use my story to help people.

I approached this goal with the same mindset that worked in fitness – put in work. I was lucky to find a writer with the same tireless tenacity that I had. In January 2017, Mike and I began meeting weekly, and hammered away at the marble block of my life, shaping it into a cohesive story to bring to the world. We pushed through, sorting through every detail, story, and stage of my life. We cranked out draft after draft until we were satisfied.

I kept going to Toastmasters to enhance my public speaking skills. Toastmasters is regimented, and uses a program to help an individual craft, develop, and deliver speeches. With the book being developed, and my public speaking skills being polished, I felt well positioned to take my message to the world. I didn't know the why yet, but in my gut, a voice reassured me it was for a righteous cause.

Midway through the process, I went to the DMV in San Pedro to renew a car registration. I took a number and sat down to read a manuscript of this book. A woman walks by me, stops, walks back, and sits down next to me. I notice everything. It's called situational awareness, and it's something that soldiers, police officers, and gang members all have in common. This woman had backtracked and sat down next to me in a room full of empty chairs. I continued to read the manuscript, but I felt her staring at me. I couldn't concentrate on reading. I finally looked up to find her eyeing me.

"You're never gonna go anywhere in life with your tattoo," she said. I wanted to whip out a reply, "Which one?" but I paused, waiting. Anyone who would go out of their way to pester someone they don't know over tattoos usually has more to say. I'm familiar with the type, the holders of moral high ground who need to let everyone know.

"That one on your head, 'Any Bitch Can Be Replaced.' How are you going to get a job or get married?" She shook her head with an extra 'oomph' noise to emphasize her disgust.

"Actually, ma'am, I am married" Saying it out loud surprised me as much as it did her.

Her face went from puzzled to curious. "What are you reading?" she asked.

"A book on my life," I replied.

Now I really had her worked up. I could see the gears in her mind turning, trying to piece all of this together.

"Why would anyone want to read a book on your life?" She pressed.

"The short of it is, I used to be in gangs, and did time in prison. I got out of prison, turned my life around and began competing in fitness. I fly all over the world to compete and tell my story. The goal is to help anyone who will listen, especially kids." I replied as patient and explanatory as I could be.

Her face lit up. She thought she found another hole. "So you waste your money and fly places, real nice."

"No, I'm paid to travel, I don't spend anything. I've represented the United States in international competitions, and won three world championships."

I had stumped her. Her quick responses ceased, and she looked at me blankly. It was uncomfortable, and then right on cue my number was called. I wished her a nice day and got out of there. On my way home I thought about the interaction. I wasn't upset, I know people are going to judge me. That's fine, I can live with it. I was trying to pull something from deep within me into my conscious mind, but I didn't know what.

Bright red brake lights of the Chevy Tahoe in front of me approached quickly. I snapped out of my trance just in time to slam on my brakes. A moment later, I would have gone through its trunk.

Then it came flying into my consciousness, jarred loose by my near accident. "The goal is to help anyone who will listen, especially kids." That's it. That is my purpose. Right there, in the middle of traffic, I leaned forward, looked up to the sky at my mother, and thanked her for showing me the path once again.

Even with her being gone, she is still doing so much for me. She did so much for everyone. I watched her help people her entire life. She watched babies, cleaned houses, gave away money, volunteered at schools – and that's just the things I witnessed. Countless acts of kindness were done when no one was watching, I am sure of that.

Now that I found my path, how much can I do with what she gave me? I want to be the flashlight that shines on the path in the woods for others. That inspiration came from watching my mother help people.

Now I had the What, and the Why. Now it's time for the How, and to put in the work. I want to talk to anyone who will listen. I want to share my struggle, tell how I clawed my way out, and inspire others to do the same. It all starts with the kids. Maybe if I can get them before they go as far as I did, I can show them that change is possible. They don't have to dig as deep as I did. It's not too late. I made a lot of bad decisions and did a lot of stupid things, but it can change if you work hard.

In late spring 2017, I found out Tasha was pregnant. Equal parts excitement and fear were fighting for power inside of me as her due date neared. There were moments I believed with a conviction clearer than anything I had felt before that everything was going to work out, followed by overwhelming fear of not wanting my son to go through the things I had to overcome.

One Saturday morning Tasha was sitting on the couch watching the news with our three dogs. I was making coffee. The landline phone rang. I picked up.

A woman's voice spoke in a robotic monotone.

"Hel-lo, you have a col-lect call from an inmate at the San Quen-tin Correctional Facility."

The robot voice cut out, and a human voice said "Johnny."

I had not heard from Johnny in years. I didn't know he was still alive. Memories came to me all at once. Playing on the schoolyard. Fighting on the schoolyard. Drinking behind the boarded up buildings on Second Street. The night in the pouring rain he stepped in front of a gun for me, and nearly had his head blown off.

I accepted the charges. Before Johnny came on the phone I heard three taps: "tsk, tsk, tsk" The prison was recording the conversation. I had not heard that sound in almost ten years.

"Hello." Johnny's raspy, but solid voice came on the line.

"What's up, man? It's been a long time. How are you doing?" I replied.

"I'm all right, man. I'm all right. Got caught up about two years back. They pinned a whole buncha shit on me. D.A. wasn't about to cut me any slack. Prolly gonna do fifteen to twenty here. I'm just maintaining, trying to keep my head up. You know how it is."

He sounded tired, but steadfast. He still had the warrior spirit in his voice, regardless of what life had thrown at him.

Tasha was staring at me with a twisted face. She had more questions than I had answers. I nodded my head to say 'I don't know either.'

"Last I seen, you were in New York doing your fitness thing, man. That's what's up," Johnny said.

"Yeah, man," I said. "I just got back from living in Dubai for five months. I was working at a gym over there. Training clients."

"Damn, homie, that's sick. What's Dubai?"

No other comment could have made me feel more different. Johnny and I grew up on the same streets. We went to the same schools, did the same drugs, hustled the same corners. But he was locked in a cage and I was staring at my wife, pregnant with our first child.

"Damn, homie. I just hope to make it outta here one day. I just want to live a normal life with a wife and kids. I ain't about this gang-banging shit anymore."

There was a long, hollow pause.

"Aight homie, I gotta go. You know we only get two minutes on here. Just wanted to say what's up. Write me sometime, homie."

"No doubt, man. Hey, keep your head up, all right?" I said.

***

Saints are admired, but rarely listened to. It's those of us who have been through hell and have found a way out who carry true wisdom, for they are keenly aware of the grace that is available to every human being.

I have come far. My journey has been long already, and it has only just started. My prior life feels like a millennium ago. In my first thirty years on this planet, I have seen more than most people see in a lifetime. I went from the same four walls of a prison cell Johnny was looking at, to seeing the world. But the hardest part of my journey is behind me. What lies ahead is a path of service and selfless giving. I am one of the lucky ones. I have lived, died, and been reborn. God looks out for his most troubled children, they are best suited to spread the most important message of humanity – hope.

About Michael Oropollo

Michael is a writer, poet, and teacher. His social and political essays have been published in the Santa Monica Daily Press and the Good Men Project, where he was a weekly columnist. He is the author of *Thoughts*, a poetry volume, and *His History, Her Story* with Dr. Debra Warner. Michael currently lives and teaches in Los Angeles, California.

CPSIA information can be obtained
at www.ICGtesting.com
Printed in the USA
BVOW09s0736200418
513783BV00018B/280/P